COOKING WITH BEER

To John—who likes his pint

CAROLE FAHY

Cooking with Beer

THE COOKERY BOOK CLUB

This edition published by
The Cookery Book Club
St Giles House, 49/50 Poland St, London W1A 2LG
by arrangement with
Elm Tree Books

Printed in Great Britain by
Western Printing Services Ltd, Bristol

Contents

Introduction   vii

Soups and Starters   1

Meat, Poultry and Game   17

Fish and Shellfish   53

Vegetables and Salads   69

Cheese and Cheese Dishes   81

Desserts   95

Baking Breads and Cakes   105

Possets, Punches and Other Beer Brews   119

Miscellaneous Recipes   129

Appendices

  I Basic Hints   137

  II Glossary of Cookery Terms   139

Index   141

The author would like to express her grateful thanks to Paul Eve for testing the recipes and to Elizabeth Kaye for typing the manuscript.

Introduction

WHEN I started this book I was amazed at the number of my friends who had never heard of cooking with beer. Most of them knew of Welsh Rarebit; a few had heard of *Carbonnades Flamandes* and one, more enterprising, had actually eaten ham boiled in beer. But that was the extent of their knowledge.

This is astonishing because we should be using our national drink to cook with as freely as we use wine. We should be doing as much to revolutionise cooking habits with beer as the French did with their national drink, because beer can have as superb an effect on the subtle flavour and consistency of our meals as any wine—and at a fraction of the cost.

Beer gives new richness and a delightful taste to a wide variety of dishes; it deliciously improves the texture and lightness of all kinds of cakes, pies and batters; has a tenderising effect on tough meats; helps preserve foods; makes bread rise; adds piquancy to dull vegetables and attractively glazes roast meats, to mention only a few of its culinary virtues.

Nor is its value restricted to a few specialised dishes. In the following pages you will find more than 300 recipes for both classic and unusual dishes cooked with beer. These cover all kinds of soups and starters; meat, poultry and game dishes; vegetables and salads; fish and shellfish dishes; cheeses and savouries; desserts (including puddings, pies and fruit sweets); breads, cakes and pastries; a miscellany of sauces and home-curing recipes and a delicious collection of possets, punches and other beer brews.

When you are using beer to cook with there are a couple of points which you should always remember. Firstly beer for cooking should be warm, never chilled. If you use chilled beer much of the flavour will be lost. Secondly it should also be slightly flat, as it is impossible to measure beer accurately when it has a 'head'. In cooking, the alcohol evaporates leaving only the delicious taste of barley and malt; so you need have no worries about giving food cooked in beer to children or even teetotallers.

There are five basic kinds of beer:

PALE ALE: A brisk, refreshing beer with an incisive hop flavour, always pale amber in colour. Pale ales include draught 'bitter' and bottled 'family', 'dinner' and 'light' ales.

MILD OR BROWN ALE: Luscious. However strong, it is always mild in flavour, being brewed with comparatively less hops and more malt and sugar. The draught X, XX or 'mild', and bottled brown ale.

STOUT: Black, robust, full-bodied, sustaining. Stouts are among the stronger beers. Some are well-hopped, which makes them taste more bitter. They are referred to in the recipes as 'stout'. Others are more lightly hopped—sweeter—and are referred to as 'sweet stout'. It is important to bear the difference in mind when following the recipes, but if in doubt as to which brand of stout to use, your supplier will advise you.

OLD ALE: Strong, mellow, satisfying. Dark in colour, every old ale has its own individuality and is subtly different from the rest in flavour. Among old ales are Burton XXXX and Scotch ales.

LAGER: In Britain, any beer of a Continental type. British lager is a delicately-flavoured, lightly-hopped beer with a creamy 'head'.

Cooking with beer is not new. Many of the recipes in this book go back to *Merrie Englande* or earlier, and some, like Buckingham-shire Florentine (a hot-ale apple pie), even retain their traditional names.

The history of beer-making goes back into antiquity. The brewing of beer is known to have been practised in Mesopotamia and Egypt at least 5,000 years ago. Egyptian records still survive showing the regulation of beer shops in 1300 BC—an early form of licensing laws. The ancient Babylonians also considered brewing a very important part of their economic and social life. They used different types of beer in their religious ceremonies and, like the Egyptians, they even designated Gods to watch over their brewing.

The Egyptians passed on their knowledge of brewing to the Greeks who in turn handed it down to the Romans, who refined the Anglo-Saxon form; for at the time of the Roman Conquest Britons were already making ale from barley and it has been the staple diet of this country ever since. For hundreds of years beer was almost the only beverage of this land and was drunk as a matter of course at all times of the day and in quantities which, to us now, would seem vast. Even women drank ale rather as they drink tea now.

In the reign of Henry VIII, maids of honour were allowed a daily ration of a gallon of ale, and Queen Elizabeth I certainly drank large quantities of a particularly strong brew. It was said to be 'so strong as there is no man able to drink it' and her household accounts show that she appeared to like nothing but bread and ale for breakfast.

English ale became the basis for many religious and social festivals. There were 'give-ales' and 'bid-ales' (rather like our church or charity fêtes nowadays), 'clerk-ales' and 'Whitsun-ales', and one which survives with almost the same name today—the 'bride-ale'.

Hops were not widely used in beer-making in this country until about 500 years ago, although hopped ale appears to have existed in Germany since Roman times and the Irsraelites are said to have protected themselves from the plague with hopped ale. When hops came into general use in England the brew was called 'biere' to distinguish it from the unhopped ale. Hops are now, of course, an essential part of English beer.

Never has there been so much interest in the arts of eating and drinking in this country as now. Gone are the days when English cooking was the joke of Europe. It is now time we left our imprint on the world of *haute cuisine* by making our national drink as common a sight in our kitchens as it undoubtedly is in our daily social life.

Soups and Starters

THE FIRST course of any meal should be delicious, light and appetising; a tantalising hint of delights to come leaving your guests hungry for the next course.

This means serving small quantities of light, tasty starters that won't fill everyone up before they sample the main course. In the following pages you will find a wide range of soups and starters made with beer, all of them a subtle and enticing beginning to any meal.

Don't be afraid to experiment with unusual starters; a wedge of beer Pipérade makes an exotic change (you'll be amazed at how cheap and simple it is to make), or surprise your guests with the excellence of your beer Quiche.

Always remember that presentation is enormously important. A soup served from a beautiful tureen or in colourful individual bowls, sprinkled with a pleasing garnish and presented with toast croûtes peeping out from a napkin, *looks* delicious—which is half the battle. A plain ungarnished effort in any old dish will probably taste as awful as it looks! And please remember, above all, that if a soup is supposed to be served hot that means really hot and if cold that means ice cold. Nothing is worse than tepid food and that applies particularly to soups, which thrive on extremes of temperature. For this reason, it is best to serve iced soups straight from the refrigerator, rather than from a tureen.

When making home-made soups it is useful to bear in mind the following rules:

(1) Never add liaison (thickening) directly to a hot soup on the stove or it will inevitably go lumpy. Pour a little of the soup into a bowl, allow to cool and then mix with the flour or eggs before stirring into the main body of the soup, off the heat.

(2) If you are making a soup which requires dried vegetables (lentils, butter beans, etc.), make sure that you soak them thoroughly overnight before use. Hard pellets sinking to the bottom of your delicately rich Vegetable Beer Soup will not do anything to improve it.

(3) When sieving soups, be certain every drop is pushed through the strainer or some of the flavour and thickness will be lost.

(4) The cooking times given for soups are minimum times and all recipes can be improved by longer cooking. Most can be made the night before and re-heated without spoiling.

Finally, if you must use a basic tinned soup for some of the mixed soups (though I don't recommend it unless you are really in a desperate rush), don't forget to follow the maker's instructions for heating through before following the recipe. By the way, if you do have an unexpected guest, almost any tinned soup is much improved by the addition of a little beer, for an unusual flavour that will disguise its origins.

Vegetable Beer Soup

2 large carrots	*2 ounces butter*
1 head celery	*½ pint split pea soup*
1 medium onion	*(preferably home-made)*
¼ pound belly of pork	*¾ pint light ale*
(cubed)	*1 cup beef stock (see p. 138)*

Scrape and dice the carrots; trim and cut the celery into 1-inch strips and peel and roughly chop the onion. Put split pea soup in a saucepan with the beer and beef stock and simmer for about 30 minutes. Meanwhile, sauté the vegetables with the belly of pork in the butter until carrots are tender. Add to the soup and leave to cook for a further 30 minutes. Serve hot.

Serves 4–6

Lentil Soup with Beer

1 cup lentils (dried)
3 pints water
½ pint lager
¼ pound belly of pork
  (cubed)
2 sticks celery
1 medium onion

a pinch thyme (dried)
1 bay leaf
1 ounce butter
1 tablespoon cornflour
black pepper (fresh ground)
grated carrot to serve

Wash and drain lentils and place these with the belly of pork in a large saucepan with the beer and water and simmer for 2–3 hours. Meanwhile, trim and chop celery into 1-inch strips, peel and dice onion and add to soup with the thyme and bay leaf for a further 30 minutes' cooking. Remove bay leaf and pork and purée soup in a blender or through a sieve. Blend liaison of butter and flour over heat in a separate pan and gradually stir in a little of the soup. Return this to the main saucepan of soup, stirring in thoroughly. Allow to simmer for a further 10 minutes. Add seasoning and serve hot with a little finely chopped grated carrot on top.

Serves 4–6

Spring Soup

½ pint stout
½ pint sour cream
2 tablespoons plain flour
1 teaspoon spring onions
  (chopped)

1 teaspoon parsley (finely
  chopped)
seasoning to taste

Blend the sour cream and flour smoothly in a saucepan. Add the spring onions, parsley and seasoning. Gradually stir in the beer over low heat. Cook until hot, without boiling, stirring all the time to prevent lumps forming. Serve hot with rounds of rye or black bread.

Serves 4

Breakfast Beer Soup

A famous beer soup, said to be a favourite dish of King Frederick
of Denmark, which he sometimes gives instead of porridge to his
guests for breakfast. The rum flavouring is an addition of the
author's.

1 thick slice rye bread per person	*2 eggs*
½ pint brown ale	*juice of ½ lemon*
¾ pint water	*whipped cream to serve*
	few drops of rum essence

Soak the rye bread in the beer until it is virtually a mash. Pour
into a large saucepan, add the water and bring slowly to the boil.
Mix in the eggs, lemon juice and flavouring. Re-heat slowly taking
care not to re-boil as this will curdle the eggs. Serve hot with a
dessertspoonful of whipped cream on the top of each bowlful.

Serves 4

Beer Bortsch

½ pound raw skirt of beef (cubed)	*½ pound tomatoes*
2 ounces streaky bacon (cubed)	*1 apple*
1 medium beetroot (raw)	*1 cup butter beans (pre-soaked or tinned)*
1 small cauliflower	*1 pint light ale*
1 large potato	*1 tablespoon castor sugar*
1 large carrot	*1 teaspoon pepper*
1 small onion	*parsley (chopped) to serve*
	cream to serve

First prepare the vegetables. Peel and shred beetroot finely; chop
cauliflower very small (using green leaves as well as flower but
not stalk); peel the tomato and leave whole; scrape and dice
carrot; peel onion and break up into natural layers; skin and
quarter tomatoes and peel, core and slice the apple. Place the
vegetables except the butter beans in a large saucepan with the
beef, bacon, sugar and seasoning. Cover with the beer, bring to
the boil and leave to simmer for about 1½ hours when vegetables

and meat should be tender. Bortsch should be of a thick consistency but not too solidly packed with vegetables, so add a little more beer if you find the liquid is vanishing in the cooking. Five minutes before the end of cooking time add the butter beans and serve with a sprinkling of chopped parsley and a spoonful of sour cream. Bortsch is usually best if it is made the day before you want to serve it. Serve hot.

Serves 4–6

Scots Pheasant Soup

1 quart game stock
carcass of 1 pheasant or any
*   game bird*
3 rashers streaky bacon
*   (cut in two)*
1 stick celery (cut into
*   1-inch strips)*
1 small turnip (diced)

1 medium sized onion
*   (diced) or 6 shallots*
¼ pint sweet stout
2–3 tablespoons port
1 wineglass tomato juice
Worcestershire sauce to
*   serve*

Have ready the game stock (*see page 138*). Do not use bouillon cubes as they are inclined to be too salty and will not give the same flavour or consistency. Break up the carcass (if there is a little meat left on it so much the better) and dry out in a medium oven at 375°F, gas mark 5, for ½ hour before putting into a large saucepan and covering with the stock. Add the vegetables, sweet stout, port, tomato juice and seasoning to taste and simmer for 3–3½ hours. From time to time skim the excess fat and scum from the top of the soup. Strain, re-heat and add Worcestershire sauce before serving. Serve hot.

Serves 4–6

French Beer Soup

¾ pint pale ale
2 ounces granulated sugar
2 egg yolks (to separate
*   from whites see p. 137)*

1 tablespoon sour cream
toast croûtes to serve

Bring the beer slowly to the boil with the sugar. Remove from heat. Pour a little into a clean mixing bowl and add to this the egg yolks and sour cream and thoroughly but gently mix together. Return contents of the bowl to the saucepan of beer and carefully re-heat to allow liaison to thicken soup. Do not allow to re-boil or eggs and cream will curdle. Serve in earthenware bowls with croûtes of dry toast.

Serves 2

Beer Soup with Prawn

½ *pint thick tomato soup*   *1 small carton single cream*
½ *pint lentil soup*   *3 ounces peeled prawns or*
½ *pint light ale*   *shrimps*

If you are in a hurry this recipe can be made very successfully with tinned, condensed soups but of course home-made are always better. Gently heat the tomato and lentil soup with the beer and the cream, taking care not to allow mixture to boil (if using condensed soups follow instructions on tin before adding cream, and beer). A few minutes before serving add the prawns and stir in thoroughly.

Serves 4

Beer Soup au Fromage

1 cup Gruyère cheese   *2 ounces chopped pimento*
  (grated)   *2 ounces clarified butter*
¾ *pint light ale*   *(see p. 139)*
1 small green pepper   *4 tablespoons cornflour*
2 small onions   ½ *pint chicken broth*
2 sticks celery   *seasoning to taste*
1 large carrot

Dice onions, carrot, celery and green pepper and cook gently in butter in the bottom of a large saucepan until tender but not brown. In a mixing bowl add a little of the cold chicken broth to the cornflour and stir till smooth. Gradually add the rest of the broth with the seasoning. Pour into the vegetable pot stirring all the time to allow flour to thicken the soup without becoming lumpy. Simmer for 20 minutes before stirring in cheese and, when cheese is melted, pour in beer and serve hot.

Serves 4

Beer Soup with Milk

1 pint brown ale
1 pint milk
2–3 egg yolks (to separate from whites see p. 137)
peel of ½ lemon (grated)

1 teaspoon cinnamon (ground)
1 ounce cornflour
2 ounces granulated sugar
½ teaspoon salt

Simmer the ale and cinnamon with the lemon peel in a large saucepan for about 15 minutes. Meanwhile, mix together the milk, egg yolks, salt and sugar and heat gently, stirring from time to time. Do not boil. Remove from heat and set aside. Mix the cornflour with about 1 cup of cold water until creamy and pour it into the hot beer mixture, stirring all the time to prevent lumps forming. Add the contents of the warm milk and re-heat soup carefully. Do not allow to boil or eggs will curdle. Serve hot.

Serves 6

Norwegian Cold Ale Soup

½ pint light ale
½ pint brown ale
juice and peel (grated) of two lemons

sugar to taste
rusks to serve
1 small orange (sliced)

Mix the ales together in a large tureen with the lemon juice, peel and sugar. Serve with rusks and half a slice of orange floating on the top. Serve cold but not iced as this would impair the flavour.

Serves 4

German Cold Ale Soup

1 quart brown ale
½ pint water
1 cup currants or sultanas
  (washed)
6 tablespoons pumpernickel
  (crumbled)

3 ounces demerara sugar
2 lemons (sliced)
1 teaspoon cinnamon
  (grated)

Pour boiling water over currants in a large soup tureen and leave
to soak for 1½–2 hours. Add the pumpernickel, sugar, lemons,
cinnamon and ale and cover. Place in the refrigerator for about
30 minutes to serve chilled.

Serves 4–6

Iced Cucumber Soup

½ pint light ale
1 large carton sour cream
2 medium cucumbers

1 teaspoon salt
½ teaspoon black pepper
  (fresh ground)

Peel and dice the cucumbers and set aside. Pour sour cream into
large soup tureen and gradually stir in the beer until it is
thoroughly mixed in. Add the cucumber and seasoning to taste
and place in the refrigerator for about 30 minutes to chill before
serving. Serve cold with croûtons.

Serves 3–4

Melon in Beer

1 medium honeydew melon
½ teaspoon cinnamon

4 tablespoons castor sugar
¼ pint light ale

Chill the melon well in the refrigerator. (If there is any other
uncovered food in the refrigerator put melon in a polythene bag
first, to prevent it flavouring other food!) Cut into four wedges;
remove seeds and sprinkle well with beer. Mix cinnamon and
sugar together in a bowl and sprinkle these over melon slices also.
Serve immediately. This recipe can be slightly varied by cutting

a hole in top of the melon, pouring in the beer and then chilling, before cutting and sprinkling with sugar and cinnamon.

Serves 4

Melon Cocktail

*1 large honeydew or
  cantaloup melon*

*1½ pints light ale
4 small sprigs mint*

Cut melon in half and remove seeds. Scoop out flesh into balls with a vegetable scoop and place them in a shallow pie-dish, or similar dish, just covering them with some of the beer. Completely cover with polythene and place in the refrigerator to chill for about 30 minutes. Meanwhile, chill remainder of the beer. When melon balls are ready put them in coupe glasses covered with 3–4 tablespoons of beer and a sprig of mint to decorate. Serve immediately.

Serves 6

Avocados Roquefort

*2 avocado pears
2 ounces Roquefort cheese
2 tablespoons lager*

*2 tablespoons French
  dressing
black pepper (fresh ground)*

Split avocados in half lengthways, removing stone. Work the cheese with the beer until smooth. Fill avocado halves with this mixture and finish off with a little French dressing and black pepper.

Serves 4

Piperade with Beer

A traditional Spanish dish to which the addition of beer gives an unusual and subtle distinction.

*3 eggs
3 egg yolks
½ cup lager
4 medium tomatoes (ripe)*

*2 red peppers
1 medium onion
2 cloves garlic
1 teaspoon garlic butter*

Break eggs and egg yolks into a bowl with the lager and beat lightly. Scald and skin tomatoes; seed and core peppers and chop both roughly with the onion. Melt a little garlic butter in a deep frying pan and sauté the tomato, pepper and onion mixture in this. Season well and cook slowly until thick and soft. Add beaten egg mixture and remaining butter to pan and stir until cooked to the consistency of scrambled egg. Pour into a flan tin to cool and set and serve cold, in wedges, with rolls. Can also be served hot.

Serves 4

Rabbit Terrine

2 pounds rabbit	*seasoning*
1 pound lean pork	*1 teaspoon brandy*
½ pint light ale	*8–10 rashers streaky bacon*

Bone rabbit and chop up pork. Place each in separate bowls and cover with beer. Add seasoning and leave to marinate overnight in the refrigerator. Drain and mince pork and rabbit separately. Line a small casserole dish, or terrine, with the rashers of bacon and layer meats alternately into this. Pour over a little beer and cover top with more bacon, some damp greaseproof paper and a lid. Cook in a bain-marie in a moderate oven, 350°F, mark 4, for 1–1½ hours. Serve cold with triangles of toast.

Serves 4–6

Beer Terrine

1 cup lager or light ale	*1 bay leaf*
4 ounces raw pork (shredded)	*1 small onion (peeled and finely chopped)*
4 ounces raw chicken (cut from the breast and shredded)	*1 teaspoon mixed dried herbs*
8 ounces lamb's liver (minced)	*¼ pint jellied stock*
8 ounces fat pork (minced)	*luting paste (see p. 139)*
8 ounces veal (minced)	*salt and pepper*

Work the minced veal, liver and fat pork in a bowl with the onion and herbs. Season this stuffing and set aside. Mix the shredded chicken and pork together. Season and cover with beer, leaving to marinate for about 20 minutes. Pour off excess beer. Pack alternate layers of shredded meat and stuffing in a terrine (or a small casserole dish with a lid) pressing down well between layers and ending with a layer of stuffing. Cover, and seal lid by running a line of luting paste round it. Cook in a bain-marie (*see* page 139) in the oven at 350°F, mark 4, for about 2 hours, until firm to the touch. When cooked remove lid and press with a heavy weight for about 2 hours. When cold remove any fat from round the sides and fill with jellied stock. Leave to set well before slicing to serve with triangles of dry toast.

Serves 6–8

Barbecued Spare Ribs in Beer

3 pounds spare ribs
1½ cups light ale
2 tablespoons honey

1 tablespoon lemon juice
1 teaspoon dry mustard

Make a marinade of the beer, honey, lemon juice and mustard. Leave ribs to soak in this in a large bowl for at least 2½ hours, or longer if possible. Pre-heat oven to 400°F, mark 6. Take ribs out of marinade and arrange in a shallow baking dish, keeping marinade aside. Place in hot oven for 15 minutes. Drain and pour 1 cup of the marinade over the ribs before returning to oven to cook for a further 45 minutes at 350°F, mark 4. Baste and turn from time to time and serve with remainder of the marinade, heated, in a sauceboat.

Serves 4

Chicory Mornay

4 heads chicory
3 tablespoons cheddar cheese
  (grated)
1 cup light ale
¼ pound ham (cooked and
  shredded)

2 ounces butter
2 ounces flour
¾ pint milk
seasoning to taste

Heat oven to 400°F, mark 6. Place chicory in a well greased casserole with the beer. Cover and heat on top of stove for about 10 minutes before putting into the oven to cook for ¾ hour, or until chicory is tender. Prepare sauce. Mix cold milk in a bowl, with the flour, a little at a time to keep it smooth, adding 2 tablespoons of the grated cheese and seasoning to taste. Melt butter in a saucepan and pour in sauce mixture. Bring to the boil, stirring continuously until sauce thickens. Mix in the shredded ham. Place chicory on a serving dish and cover with sauce, dusting top with remaining cheese. Pop under grill for a few minutes to brown.

Serves 4

Quiche Lorraine à la Bière

1 egg
1 egg yolk
1 medium onion
6 rashers streaky bacon
*2 tablespoons Cheddar
   cheese (grated)*
¼ cup light ale

1 cup milk
*8 ounces shortcrust pastry
   for flan case (frozen—or
   homemade, see p. 138)*
1 ounce butter
seasoning to taste

Roll out pastry to ¼ inch thick and line into flan case. Dice bacon rashers and slice onion into rings and sauté together in butter in a frying pan, until onion is soft but not brown. Meanwhile, mix egg, extra yolk, milk and beer together in a bowl with the grated cheese. Pour contents of sauté pan (including what remains of the butter) into the other ingredients and mix well together. Pour into flan case, making sure that bacon and onion are fairly evenly distributed, and bake in a moderate oven, 350°F, mark 4, for 25–30 minutes.

Serves 4

Poached Eggs with Beer Sauce

6 eggs
3 baps
1 cup single cream
¼ pint light ale

2 tablespoons horseradish
1 rasher streaky bacon
1 spring onion
seasoning to taste

Poach eggs in the usual way until white is set. Slice baps and place one egg on each half. Grill bacon, dice with spring onion and set aside. Mix beer, cream and horseradish together and pour a little of this sauce over each egg. Sprinkle eggs with bacon and spring onion and place on a baking sheet under the grill to re-heat.

Serves 6

Beer Omelet (1)

1 slice white bread
½ cup light ale
5 eggs
2 tablespoons butter

1 tablespoon parsley
    (finely chopped)
seasoning

Dice the bread and soak in the light ale until very soft. Break eggs into a bowl and beat lightly with seasoning to taste. Gradually stir in the bread mixture and beat until frothy. Melt half the butter in a very hot omelet pan and pour in half the egg mixture. Cook in the usual way (*see* page 138) and sprinkle finished omelet with parsley. Repeat with remaining mixture for second omelet.

Serves 2

Beer Omelet (2)

½ cup light ale
4 eggs
2 tablespoons Cheddar cheese
    (grated)

1 ounce butter

Lightly beat the eggs with the beer in a mixing bowl. Heat an omelet pan until it is really hot and drop in half the butter. Pour in half the egg mixture and fork around until fluffy (*see* omelet rules page 138) before covering with half the grated cheese. Fold over and leave to cook for a few seconds to allow cheese to melt before turning out on to a hot plate. Repeat for second omelet.

Serves 2

Eggs Baked in Beer

6 eggs
2 ounces butter
¾ cup sweet stout
1 medium onion
½ red pepper

1 cup breadcrumbs
  (browned—see p. 137)
1 cup Cheddar cheese
  (grated)
seasoning to taste

Peel onions and dice with peppers. Sauté in butter in a frying pan until soft. Turn into a casserole dish and break eggs one at a time on top. Cover with crumbs and grated cheese and add the beer. Place in pre-heated low oven, 325°F, mark 3, for about 30 minutes or until whites are set.

Serves 3

Hot Shrimps Hors d'Oeuvres

½ pound raw shrimps
  (shelled and de-veined)
½ pint light ale
2 tablespoons onion
  (chopped)
2 ounces butter
1 teaspoon salt

¼ teaspoon Tabasco sauce
2 dessertspoons flour
2 tablespoons lemon juice
1 bay leaf
2 teaspoons parsley (finely
  chopped)

Melt butter in a frying pan and sauté onion and shrimps together in this for a couple of minutes. Add salt, Tabasco sauce, and flour. Slowly mix in flour and salt and gradually add beer stirring all the time. Add remaining ingredients and bring to the boil. To serve discard bay leaf and sprinkle with parsley. Serve on buttered toast.

Serves 6

Shrimp Vol-au-Vents

½ cup lager
½ pound raw shrimps
   (peeled)
½ pound cottage cheese
1 tablespoon olives
   (chopped)

1 tablespoon parsley
   (finely chopped)
4–6 large vol-au-vent cases
   (bought or homemade)
paprika to serve

First have ready, or make, the vol-au-vent cases. Pre-heat oven to
350°F, mark 4. Mix the shrimps in a bowl with the cream cheese
and gradually work in the beer and olives. Fill vol-au-vent cases
with this mixture and set on a baking sheet, with pastry 'hats' laid
separately, to cook for 10–15 minutes. When heated through, dust
with paprika before covering with 'hats' to serve immediately.

Serves 4

Meat, Poultry and Game

MEAT COOKED in beer takes on a new and subtle flavour and benefits from the amazing tenderising properties of the brew. The toughest piece of meat will melt in the mouth if you marinate it overnight in beer before cooking. Roast meat basted with beer will also acquire an attractive glaze.

Beef is probably the meat most commonly cooked in beer, perhaps because the Belgian National dish of *Carbonnades Flamandes* is so well known and has given rise to so many variations. But, in fact, just about any meat, poultry or game can be improved by cooking in beer.

In this chapter you will find recipes covering all kinds of meat and offal, poultry and game; cooked in a variety of ways from roasts and sautés to casseroles and stews. Many of these dishes call for basting and you will find that it pays to take care how you carry out this apparently easy task.

To baste a joint properly you should take the baking tin, or casserole dish, out of the oven (closing the door to keep the temperature constant) and spoon the hot liquid, or fat, several times over the meat. If you are turning roast meat take care not to spear it with a fork or knife as this will make the juices run out, losing some of the flavour and succulence.

Poultry properly trussed will cook better and have a nicer appearance as the breast meat will be plumped up, stuffing will be secured in place and the bird will cook more evenly. Correct carving is important, too, particularly with duck.

When choosing poultry, remember that fresh birds should be creamy in colour and have a plump breast. Don't choose birds that look at all bluish. Frozen birds should be thawed in a cool place for 24 hours—never thaw under a hot tap as this toughens the meat.

If you are making a sauté or casserole you will find that jointing poultry and game yourself is more satisfactory than buying ready-cut pieces as they tend to have too much bone left in. Remember that all game needs hanging for flavour and tenderness but the length of time you hang it depends upon individual taste. If you are going to hang game yourself, do not pluck or draw it until you are ready to use it.

Finally, you will find rabbit and pigeon recipes in the game section of this chapter, although, strictly speaking, they are not game. They are, however, usually sold on the same counter, and are classified as game for convenience.

Carbonnade (1)

2 pounds raw beef steak	1 tablespoon flour
2 tablespoons butter	½ pint sweet stout
2 tablespoons olive oil	seasoning to taste
4 onions	

Heat olive oil in a heavy frying pan. Slice beef and brown on both sides. Turn contents of pan into a casserole. Peel and slice onions thinly and sauté in butter in the frying pan. Sprinkle with flour and add to meat in casserole. Season to taste. Cover with sweet stout and, with the lid on, cook over a low flame for about 2 hours, or until beef is tender. Serve with creamed potatoes and braised celery.

Serves 4

Carbonnade (2)

4 pounds beef	½ pint boiling water
½ pound green bacon	¾ pint sweet stout
2 tablespoons each butter and	2 tablespoons mixed herbs
olive oil	4 tablespoons white wine
3 Spanish onions	vinegar
seasoned flour	

Cut beef into large cubes and roll in seasoned flour. Dice bacon and sauté in butter and olive oil in a frying pan. Transfer bacon to a large casserole leaving fats in pan and brown the meat in this. Turn into casserole. Peel and slice onions and sauté in remaining fat until soft and add to casserole. Pour off excess fat from pan and de-glaze with boiling water. Pour over casserole. Add beer and herbs; cover and cook in a pre-heated low oven, 300°F, mark 2, for about 2½ hours. Stir in vinegar before serving.

Serves 6–8

Stewed Steak Chasseur

1 pound best stewing steak	*2 ounces butter*
1 large onion	*1 pint brown ale*
¼ pound mushrooms (large, flat kind)	*1 stick celery*
	1 tablespoon seasoned flour
3 rashers back bacon	*seasoning to taste*

Peel and roughly chop mushrooms and onion. Trim and dice celery. Sauté celery and onion together with half the butter in one pan and bacon and mushrooms together with remaining butter in another, until onion is soft and bacon crisp. Cut stewing steak into large chunks and roll in seasoned flour. Pile into a casserole dish with the vegetables and bacon. Cover with stock and ale and season to taste. Cook in a moderate oven, 325°F, mark 3, for 2½–3 hours. Serve with jacket potatoes.

Serves 2

Beef and Mustard Casserole

1½ pounds shin of beef	*pinch of brown sugar*
½ ounce plain flour	*dash of vinegar*
1 ounce dripping	*slices white bread as required*
3 onions (chopped)	*3 teaspoons English mustard (made)*
½ pint stock (see p. 138)	
½ pint brown ale	*seasoning to taste*
pinch of nutmeg (grated)	

Peel and chop onions and sauté in the dripping. Cut beef into cubes and roll in flour. Place in a large saucepan with the onions, stock, beer, nutmeg, sugar, vinegar and seasoning. Bring to the boil and turn into a casserole to cook in a moderate oven, 325°F, mark 3, for about 2 hours or until meat is very tender. Remove crusts from bread, cut into large squares and spread with mustard. Place in casserole, mustard side down, and cook uncovered for a further ½ hour.

Serves 4

Farmhouse Casserole

1½ *pounds skirt of beef*
  (*thickly sliced*)
4 *medium onions*
4 *large carrots*
½ *pound button mushrooms*
1 *pound tomatoes*
½ *pint light ale*

1 *stick celery*
bouquet garni
1 *bay leaf*
2 *ounces butter*
2 *tablespoons tomato paste*
seasoning

Peel and rougly chop onions. Trim and cut celery into 1-inch strips. Peel and trim mushrooms and sauté all these together in the butter. When onions are soft, pile into a casserole with the beef. Cover with the beer; stir in tomato paste. Season well and drop in bouquet garni and bay leaf. Leave to cook in a moderate oven, 350°F, mark 4, for at least 2½–3 hours.

Serves 4

Stewed Beef in Beer

1 *pound best stewing steak*
2 *medium onions*
½ *pint beef stock* (see
  p. 138)
½ *pint sweet stout*
1 *teaspoon mixed dried*
  herbs

1 *teaspoon salt*
½ *teaspoon black pepper*
  (*fresh ground*)
2 *ounces butter*
2 *ounces plain flour*

Peel and thinly slice the onions. Cut meat into 4 equal pieces. Sauté onions in the butter until soft but not brown and layer into a casserole with the beef. Smooth the flour into the butter left in the sauté pan and gradually add stock, beer, herbs and seasoning; stirring all the time to prevent lumps forming. Bring to the boil and pour over contents of casserole. Cover and leave to cook in a low oven 300°F, mark 2, for 3 hours.

Serves 2

Beef Marinated in Beer

4 pounds beef (rump or round)
4 tablespoons olive oil
2 tablespoons soft brown sugar

2 tablespoons flour
1 wineglass red wine
½ pint double cream

MARINADE

½ pint light ale
1 pint water
4 tablespoons olive oil
1 Spanish onion (peeled and sliced)

6 medium carrots (sliced)
2 bay leaves
6 peppercorns

First make beer marinade by mixing together marinade ingredients. Soak beef in this (in the refrigerator) for 48 hours, turning meat once or twice a day. Remove meat from marinade and drain, reserving marinade. Heat olive oil in a casserole dish just large enough to hold beef. Add meat and brown all over. Pour ½ pint of marinade, with vegetables and seasonings, over meat. Cover casserole and cook for 1¾ hours in a very slow oven 300°F, mark 2, adding more marinade liquid during cooking if necessary. Remove casserole from oven; sprinkle meat with brown sugar and simmer on top of the stove, uncovered, for 15 minutes longer, turning meat until sugar has melted and browned. Stir flour into remaining marinade juices. Add red wine and pour over meat. Roast, uncovered, for 30 minutes, or until sauce thickens. Strain; skim fat. Stir in cream and pour over meat. Serve immediately with château potatoes and French beans.

Serves 6–8

Steak and Kidney Pudding

8 ounces suet crust pastry
  (see p. 138)
1 pound stewing steak
1 medium sized onion
  (finely chopped)

4 ounces ox kidney
2 tablespoons seasoned flour
1 teaspoon dry mustard
3 tablespoons light ale

Have ready suet crust pastry and roll out ⅔ to ¼ inch thick. Line this into a well-greased pudding basin. Cut steak into 1-inch cubes and roll in seasoned flour and dry mustard. Split, skin and slice kidneys and roll in seasoned flour and mustard. Peel and dice onion and layer all into pudding. Add the beer. Roll out remaining pastry to form top. Place it over pudding and seal the edges with cold water. Cover with greaseproof paper and a large piece of pleated aluminium foil, secured round the sides with string, and leave to steam for 3½ to 4 hours.

Serves 4

Brewer's Pot Roast

4–5 pounds pot roast of beef
2 tablespoons English
  mustard (made)
seasoning to taste

2 tablespoons oil
1 large onion (sliced)
½ pint light ale
1 cup sour cream

Spread meat with mustard and sprinkle over seasoning. Heat oil in a flameproof dish and brown beef all over quickly. Add onion and a little beer and simmer for 3 to 4 hours, adding beer at intervals. Roast should be just covered with liquid. Skim fat and stir sour cream into liquid, mixing well, just before serving. Serve with braised celery, glazed carrots and potatoes of your choice.

Serves 6

Charlie's Rump Steak

4 pieces thick rump steak	1 bay leaf
½ pint light ale	1 clove
2 tablespoons butter	2 tablespoons tomato paste
¾ cup plain flour	6 potatoes (peeled and
2 teaspoons salt	halved)
½ teaspoon black pepper	12 small white onions
¼ teaspoon garlic salt	(peeled)

Season steak with salt, pepper and garlic salt and roll in flour. Melt butter in a large pan and 'flame' meat on both sides quickly. Add beer, bay leaf and clove and stir in tomato paste. Cover and simmer for 1 hour. Add potatoes and onions and cook covered for a further ½ hour.

Serves 4

Chilli Casserole

3 pounds brisket of beef	2 onions (sliced)
1 pint brown ale	2 sticks celery (trimmed
1 teaspoon salt	and sliced)
½ teaspoon pepper	¼ cup water
2 tablespoons chilli sauce	¼ cup parsley (chopped)

Place the meat in a casserole dish with seasoning, chilli sauce, onion and celery. Add water and cook uncovered at 350°F, mark 4, until brown. Add beer and continue cooking for about 3 hours. Remove meat. Strain the gravy, and add the parsley. Slice the meat thinly and serve in the gravy with braised carrots and château potatoes.

Serves 4

Biftek à la Bière

2–2½ pounds thick rump steak	1 pound button mushrooms
2 ounces butter	1 tablespoon lemon juice
1 clove garlic	1 tablespoon flour
4 tablespoons olive oil	½ pint brown ale
	1 teaspoon chilli sauce

Chop clove of garlic finely, sprinkle over steak and press into meat. Brush with olive oil and season. Leave for 1½ hours to absorb flavour. Peel and slice mushrooms and sauté in butter and lemon juice until soft. Mix flour with a little of the beer until smooth and add to sauté pan with rest of the beer. Add remaining garlic and chilli sauce. Keep warm and grill steak to required rareness before covering with sauce. Serve with French fried potatoes and broccoli.

Serves 4

German Rump Steak with Beer

1½ pounds rump steak	½ pint water
½ pound streaky bacon rashers (green)	3 tablespoons vinegar
	1 tablespoon treacle
2 medium onions (peeled and sliced)	6 black peppercorns
	2 cloves
1 pint sweet stout	seasoning to taste

Beat the steak with a meat bat and roll up. Tie with string. Line a casserole dish with rashers of bacon and cover with sliced onion. Lay the meat on top. Add beer and water (which should cover roll) then pour over vinegar. Season to taste. Add treacle, peppercorns and 2 cloves. Cover and simmer for 3 hours, turning occasionally. Cook in a slow oven, 300°F, mark 2, for 3 hours. To serve, remove string and garnish with green peas, glazed carrots and bacon and onion.

Serves 3

Steak in Ale

1½ pounds rump steak	½ pint light ale
2 ounces butter	1 tablespoon cornflour
2 large Spanish onions	a little cold water
seasoning to taste	

Peel and slice onions and sauté in butter in a large frying pan. When soft but not brown turn into a shallow saucepan. Season steak and place over the onion. Cover and cook over the lowest heat for 2 hours. Pour in beer. Cover and simmer for another 2 hours. Mix cornflour with water to a smooth paste and stir into gravy to thicken. Serve with new potatoes.

Serves 3–4

Pot Roast of Beef

4 pounds round of beef	1 teaspoon caraway seeds
3 pints brown ale	1 tablespoon butter
2 glasses red wine	1 dessertspoon flour
1 teaspoon made mustard	seasoning to taste

Place beef in a deep basin. Mix the ale with the wine; pour over the meat, and add enough cold water to cover. Season to taste. Soak for 12 hours, then drain reserving marinade. Brush with melted butter. Place in a casserole dish and bake in a hot oven, 450°F, mark 8, till brown all over, turning when the top is well done. Mix mustard and caraway seeds, and sprinkle over the top of the meat. Strain in 1 pint of the marinade. Cover and bake in a slow oven 275–300°F, mark 1–2, until meat is tender (about 3 hours) turning at half-time, and basting. Melt butter in a small saucepan and stir in flour. Stir over low heat until brown, then gradually add stock from pot roast, stirring constantly. Season to taste. Dish up meat and pour gravy into a sauceboat. Serve pot roast with boiled potatoes, boiled onions and Brussels sprouts.

Serves 4–6

Stewed Steak and Mushrooms

2 pounds best stewing steak	2 medium carrots
1 pint light ale	1 stick celery
2 ounces bacon fat (cut into larding strips)	¼ pound mushrooms (the large flat kind)
6 rashers streaky bacon	1 teaspoon lemon rind (grated)
1 large onion	

Wipe and beat the steak with a meat bat and lard with the bacon fat, cut in tiny strips (*see* page 139). Peel and slice onion; scrape and slice carrots; trim and dice celery and peel and slice mushrooms. Line a casserole with the bacon rashers and place half the vegetables on top. Arrange meat over the vegetables; cover with mushroom slices and remainder of vegetables. Season to taste and sprinkle with lemon rind and add light ale. Cover and cook in a slow oven 300°F, mark 2, for 2½–3 hours. Dish up meat. Mix flour to a paste with cold water and stir into gravy to thicken over heat. Serve with boiled or creamed potatoes.

Serves 6–8

Steak and Kidney Pie

1½ pounds best stewing steak
2 kidneys
¼ pint Scots ale
¼ pint of beef stock (see
  p. 138)
1 medium onion
1 tablespoon seasoned flour
  (see p. 139)

8 ounces plain flour
3 ounces lard
3 ounces butter
½ cup cold water
½ cup hot water
1 egg (beaten)

As the pastry for this recipe takes a long time to prepare, it is best to make it well in advance and leave it in the refrigerator until you are ready to use it. First prepare the flaky pastry. Cut butter into two pieces and lard into two pieces. Sift flour into a mixing bowl and rub one piece of lard into it then mix to a firm dough with a little cold water. Knead dough and roll out to an oblong. Cut one portion of butter into small pieces and dot over dough. Fold in three (like an envelope) and roll out again. Repeat this last twice, using lard and butter alternately. Do not roll out on last time but place in refrigerator to chill for about 20 minutes in a polythene bag. Roll out again and dot with last portion of butter, fold again and roll out for last time to ¼ inch thick. Line half the pastry into a well-greased pie dish.

Cut meat into cubes, roll in seasoned flour and peel and dice onion. Split, skin and slice kidneys. Layer all these ingredients into the dish around a pie funnel. Pour over stock and ale and season. Roll out remaining pastry to ¼ inch thick and cut two long narrow strips, the width of the edge of the pie dish. Seal these onto pastry round the edge of the dish. Cover pie with pastry, sealing and fluting edges and make a hole for pie funnel to 'breathe'. Brush with beaten egg. Bake for about 30 minutes in a pre-heated oven at 425°F, mark 7; wrap pie in damp grease-proof paper to prevent pastry burning during remainder of cooking. Turn heat down to 325°F, mark 3, and cook for another 1½ hours. Meanwhile, make a decoration out of the pastry trimmings, to cover the funnel hole when serving. Bake for 15–20 minutes on a baking tray in the oven during the last stage of pie cooking. When pie is ready to serve, cut first portion and quickly pour a little boiling water into pie to dilute the very concentrated gravy. Serve with creamed potatoes and Brussels sprouts.

Serves 4

Goulash with Beer

1 pound skirt of beef (raw)	*⅓ cup brown ale*
2 medium onions	*2 tablespoons tomato paste*
2 ounces clarified butter	*1 tablespoon vinegar*
(see p. 139)	*1 tablespoon lemon rind*
1 tablespoon paprika	*juice 1 lemon*
½ cup beef stock (see p. 138)	*4 rashers bacon*

Peel and dice the onion and sauté in a frying pan with half the clarified butter. Meanwhile, cut meat into large cubes and when onion is soft, but not brown, turn with contents of frying pan into a large saucepan. Stir in paprika and leave to 'flame' for a few moments. Add stock and bring to the boil. Stir in tomato paste, beer, vinegar and lemon juice and leave to simmer for 2½–3 hours, until meat is really tender and liquid has reduced to a rich gravy. If liquid seems to be disappearing too fast add a little more beer from time to time. Grate lemon rind and cut bacon into 1-inch strips: sauté together in remains of clarified butter until bacon is crisp. Sprinkle on top of goulash as a garnish. Serve with buttered egg noodles and boiled potatoes.

Serves 2

Beer Burgers

1 pound beef (minced)	*½ cup light ale*
½ medium onion (finely	*seasoning to taste*
chopped)	*dash Worcestershire sauce*
½ cup plain flour	

Mix the mince thoroughly with the onion, seasoning and Worcestershire sauce. Shape into thick burgers and roll in flour. Melt butter in a frying pan and sprinkle with Worcestershire sauce. Make a hole in the top of each hamburger and fill with beer. Place in pan and fry. Beer will be absorbed into the hamburger by the time you are ready to cook the second side. Turn and cook second side to required rareness.

Serves 4

Savoury Meat Loaf

1 pound beef (minced) *2 ounces butter*
1 egg *1 tablespoon onion (finely*
1 cup light ale *chopped)*
1½ cups breadcrumbs *½ teaspoon thyme*
(soft—see p. 137) *2 tablespoons chilli sauce*

Beat egg lightly in a bowl; add 3 tablespoons beer, breadcrumbs, onion, thyme, seasoning and meat. Mix thoroughly together and shape into a loaf. Melt butter in a flameproof dish and brown loaf on all sides. Add remaining beer and simmer, covered for 25 minutes. Just before serving stir in chilli sauce and heat through again.

Serves 4

Meatballs with Beer

1 pound beef (minced) *1 tablespoon oil*
½ pound pork sausage meat *1 tablespoon flour*
¾ pint brown ale *1 clove garlic (crushed)*
2 tablespoons onion (finely *1 teaspoon dried dill*
chopped) *(crushed)*
1 egg *seasoning to taste*
½ cup tomato purée

Lightly beat egg and mix in a bowl with meat, onion and seasoning. Shape into meat balls. Brown in the oil in a frying pan. Remove from pan and set aside. Blend flour smoothly into oil left in pan and gradually add beer, stirring continuously to prevent lumps forming. Add tomato purée and herbs and return meatballs to pan to reheat in this sauce. Makes a delicious spaghetti sauce.

Serves 4

New World Ribs

3–4 pounds lean beef ribs	*1 teaspoon salt*
2 tablespoons flour	*1 cup light ale*
1 teaspoon paprika	*1 teaspoon caraway seeds*

Mix flour, paprika and salt together. Cut beef into ribs and roll in this mixture. Arrange in a baking dish and bake at 450°F, mark 8, for 25 minutes. Meanwhile, mix tomato sauce with the beer and caraway seeds. Pour over the meat and lower oven to 325°F, mark 2–3, and continue cooking for another 1½ hours. Serve with egg noodles.

Serves 4

Frankfurters in Beer Sauce (1)

2 pounds Frankfurter	*1 tablespoon brown sugar*
sausages	*1 tablespoon cornflour*
½ pint light ale	*1 tablespoon parsley*
½ medium onion (chopped)	*(finely chopped)*
¼ teaspoon black pepper	
(fresh ground)	

Pour beer into a large saucepan with the onion, pepper, and brown sugar. Simmer sausages in this mixture for 20 minutes. Mix cornflour with a little cold water and add to saucepan, stirring all the time to thicken sauce. Serve hot in a chafing dish sprinkled with parsley. Ideal for a party dish.

Serves 12

Frankfurters in Beer Sauce (2)

8 Frankfurters	*3 cloves*
2 cups brown ale	*1 tablespoon lemon juice*
1 tablespoon brown sugar	*seasoning to taste*

Place Frankfurters in deep frying pan, pour beer over, adding brown sugar, cloves and seasoning. Boil for 10 minutes. Remove from heat and add lemon juice. Serve hot with boiled potatoes.

Serves 3–4

Frankfurters and Sauerkraut

2 pounds Frankfurters   *10 peppercorns*
2 pounds sauerkraut (tinned)   *1 tart apple (peeled and*
1 pint light ale   *sliced)*
1 small onion (chopped)   *2 cloves*
1 ounce butter

Drain sauerkraut. Place in a large saucepan with enough beer to cover, reserving at least 1 cup of beer. Sauté onion in butter and add to sauerkraut with peppercorns and apple. Cover and simmer for $\frac{1}{2}$ hour. Cook Frankfurters in boiling water for 5 minutes and drain. Add remaining beer and cloves; cover and cook for another 10 minutes. Serve sauerkraut heaped up on plates with Frankfurters on top.

Serves 6

Beef Sausage Alsace

1 pound large beef sausages   *1 tablespoon plain flour*
2 ounces butter   *1 red cabbage*
2 large onions   *1 tablespoon brown sugar*
1 bay leaf   *2 tablespoons vinegar*
1 pint brown ale

Shred the cabbage and place in a large saucepan with just enough water to cover. Add sugar and vinegar and bring to the boil. Simmer for 20–30 minutes, or until tender, taking care to add a little more water if liquid is boiling away. Meanwhile, place sausages in a bowl and scald with boiling water. Drain and dry. Brown in butter in the frying pan. Peel and slice onions and add to pan with bay leaf. Add half the ale and bring to the boil. When well reduced pour in remaining ale. Mix cornflour with a little cold water to a smooth paste and stir in to thicken sauce. Remove bay leaf and dish up with red cabbage.

Serves 3–4

Beer and Sausage Casserole

1 pound beef sausages	*3 large cooking apples*
2 ounces beef dripping	*½ pint sweet stout*
2 medium onions	*seasoning to taste*

Lightly brown sausages in dripping in a frying pan. Meanwhile, peel, core and slice apples into rings, peel and thinly slice onions. Cut browned sausages in halves and turn into a casserole, layering with onions and apples alternately. Cover with stout and cook in a moderate oven, 350°F, mark 4, for about 40 minutes. Serve with creamed potatoes.

Serves 3–4

Spicy Sausages

1 pound pork sausages	*1 bay leaf*
½ pint brown ale	*3 peppercorns*
1 ounce lard	*1 clove*

Fry sausages in the lard until brown. Drain fat and pour over beer with bay leaf, clove and peppercorns. Bring to the boil and simmer for about 15–20 minutes. Serve with braised cabbage and creamed potatoes.

Serves 4

Braised Pork in Beer

2 pounds shoulder of pork	*1 bay leaf*
1 pint light ale	*½ teaspoon thyme*
2 pounds onions	*small tin red kidney beans*
2 ounces butter	

Melt butter in a frying pan. Peel and slice onions and cut pork into chunks and brown all over with the onions in the butter. Add bay leaf, thyme and beer. Cover and simmer for 1½ to 2 hours. About 10 minutes before end of cooking time, add red kidney beans. Serve with new boiled potatoes.

Serves 4

Pork Casserole

1½ pounds pork (cooked and
    cut into pieces)
½ pint brown ale
1 small onion
2 sticks celery

1 ounce butter
1½ cups black breadcrumbs
½ teaspoon brown sugar
seasoning to taste

Peel and chop onion and trim and chop celery. Sauté together in a frying pan in butter. Add pork and mix. In a casserole dish combine beer, breadcrumbs, sugar and seasoning. Add meat and vegetables and cover. Cook in the oven at 375°F, mark 5, for about 40 minutes.

Serves 4

Pork Chops with Sauerkraut

1 pound sauerkraut (pre-
    cooked or tinned)
2 cups light ale
4 large pork chops
1 teaspoon salt

1 teaspoon black pepper
1 clove garlic (minced)
2 apples
1 cup potato (grated)
1 ounce butter

Heat sauerkraut in a large saucepan with 1 cup of light ale. Peel, core and chop apples. Season pork chops to taste and sauté lightly on both sides in butter in a frying pan. Place half the sauerkraut on the bottom of a casserole dish, season and sprinkle with garlic. Lay chops over sauerkraut and cover with a layer of apples then potato and the remaining sauerkraut on top. Sprinkle last cup of beer over and cover. Cook in a moderate oven, 350°F, mark 4, for about 45 minutes or until chops are tender.

Serves 4

Pork Fillets in Brown Ale

2 large pork fillets
½ pint brown ale
¼ teaspoon basil (crushed)
1 bay leaf

1½ cups breadcrumbs
1 egg
seasoning to taste

Place the pork fillets in a flameproof casserole dish with the bay leaf, basil, beer and seasoning. Bring to the boil, cover and simmer for about ¾ hour. Meanwhile, beat egg on a large plate and shake breadcrumbs onto a clean surface. Remove pork fillets from casserole and leave to cool for a few minutes. Dip both sides of fillets in egg and then in crumbs, pressing crumbs firmly on with a knife. Place in a shallow baking dish and baste with a little of the liquid left in the casserole dish. Heat oven to 400°F, mark 5, and bake for about 20 minutes, basting frequently with stock from casserole.

Serve with creamed potatoes and green peas.

Serves 2

Roast Pork in Beer and Herbs

4 pound piece of roasting pork (without crackling)
1 clove garlic
½ teaspoon rosemary
juice 1 lemon

1 cup lager
1 tablespoon brown sugar
seasoning to taste
2 ounces butter—clarified (see p. 139)

Chop garlic into slivers and stick into meat all round. Set in a baking tin. Heat butter in a pan and mix in rosemary, lemon juice and lager. Heat gently and spoon over meat. Pre-heat oven to 400°F, mark 6. Sprinkle sugar on top of roast and cook for 20 minutes. Turn heat down to 350°F, mark 4, and continue cooking for another 1¼–1½ hours, or until meat is cooked through, basting frequently. Serve with roast potatoes and vegetables of your choice.

Serves 6

Pork Chops in Ale

4 pork chops
½ pint light ale
3 medium onions
¼ pint chicken stock (see p. 138)

bouquet garni
1 tablespoon plain flour
3 large apples
seasoning to taste

Place pork chops in a casserole dish and cover with the beer. Leave to marinate for about 1 hour. Peel and slice onions in rings and sauté in butter in a frying pan. Lay onion rings over pork chops, pour on stock and add bouquet garni and seasoning. Cover and cook in a moderate oven 350°F, mark 4, for 1½–2 hours or until meat is tender. Meanwhile, peel and slice apples into rings and sauté lightly. Add to casserole just before serving.

Serves 4

Sweet Boiled Ham (1)

3 pounds boiling ham	*½ teaspoon salt*
1 tablespoon honey	*½ teaspoon ginger (ground)*
¼ pint sweet stout	*4 apples (unpeeled)*
1 tablespoon sherry	

Make a marinade of the beer, honey, sherry, salt and ginger and steep ham in this overnight in the refrigerator. Remove from marinade and place in a baking tin with a little of the liquid. Pre-heat oven to 350°F, mark 4, and roast for about 1½ hours or until ham is cooked through. Baste frequently. Core, but do not peel apples and bake separately for about 35–40 minutes. Baste them from time to time with some of the marinade. Serve ham with apples, boiled onions and potatoes in white sauce.

Serves 4

Sweet Boiled Ham (2)

3 pounds boiling ham	*3 medium carrots*
1 pint brown ale	*3 sticks celery*
½ pint Marsala	*1 large cabbage*
½ cup brown sugar	*3 medium onions*
3 tablespoons black treacle	

Soak ham in cold water overnight. Drain and place in a large saucepan with the beer, Marsala, black treacle and brown sugar. Scrape and slice carrots; trim and halve celery sticks; peel onions and leave whole. Add these vegetables to the pot and bring to the boil. Simmer for about 1½ hours or until ham is cooked through. Half an hour before end of cooking time add cabbage, cut into four. Serve with boiled potatoes, cooked separately.

Serves 3

Baked Ham with Pineapple

5–6 pounds boiling ham
1 onion (peeled and halved)
1 bay leaf
2 tablespoons soft brown
   sugar

½ pint sweet stout
small tin pineapple slices
black grapes

Place ham in a saucepan and cover with cold water. Cover and bring to the boil. Skim well, add onion and bay leaf. Bring again to the boil and simmer for 40–45 minutes. Remove, drain and carefully remove skin. Place the ham in a roasting tin, fat upwards, and sprinkle a good layer of brown sugar all over it. Pour the stout into the tin and bake at 450°F, mark 7–8, for 15 minutes to caramelise the sugar. Lower heat to 350°F, mark 4. Arrange pineapple rings over the sugar, sticking them in place with cocktail sticks, sprinkle with more sugar and baste with the stout. Cook for a further 15 minutes per pound, basting occasionally. Place grapes in the centre of each pineapple slice for the last 10–15 minutes. Remove meat to a hot dish. Pour ¼ pint of the liquid in which the ham was boiled into the tin, bring to the boil and allow to bubble furiously until it is reduced by about one-third. Serve this sauce separately.

Serves 4

Sweet Boiled Bacon

2½ pound joint of forehock
   of bacon
1 tablespoon black treacle
1 bay leaf

1 pint light ale
1 tablespoon black pepper
   (fresh ground)
1 tablespoon cornflour

Soak the joint in cold water for four hours. Remove the rind. Place in a large saucepan with the bay leaf and season with pepper. Spoon the treacle over the bacon fat. Pour over beer.

Cover and simmer gently for two hours. Remove bacon and keep hot. Mix a little of the juice, off the heat, with the cornflour and return to main liquid. Bring to the boil, stirring constantly to prevent lumps forming. Serve with new potatoes, boiled onions and carrots, with liquid as a separate sauce.

Serves 4

Gammon Casserole

2 thick slices gammon
1½ pounds potatoes
¼ pint light ale
1 tablespoon plain flour

½ cup Cheddar cheese
　(grated)
½ pint milk
seasoning to taste

Peel and slice potatoes and layer into the bottom of a well-buttered casserole dish. Blend flour and butter in a saucepan and gradually add milk, stirring continuously to thicken without lumps. Stir in cheese until melted. Season and pour over potato slices. Place gammon on top and cover. Cook in a slow oven, 300°F, mark 2, for about 1½ hours or until tender, basting from time to time with light ale.

Serves 2

Gammon Steaks Veronique

2 gammon steaks
¼ pint lager
1 dessertspoon English
　mustard (made)

1 tablespoon brown sugar
small bunch white grapes
1 ounce butter

Melt butter in a frying pan. Flame gammon steaks for a few seconds in this. Pour over lager. Cover and simmer for 5 minutes. Remove gammon steaks from liquid; spread with mustard and sprinkle over sugar. Finish cooking under grill. Meanwhile, peel, halve and de-pip enough grapes to garnish. Garnish gammon with grapes and serve with sauté potatoes.

Serves 2

Roast Leg of Lamb

1 leg lamb   *1 wineglass port*
1 clove garlic   *½ pint brown stock (see p.*
olive oil   *138)*
½ pint stout   *seasoning*

Rub the meat all over with a cut clove of garlic. Brush with olive oil and season. Place in a roasting dish and pour the stout over the meat, then roast for 20 minutes per pound in a moderate oven, 350°F, mark 4, basting frequently with stout. Just before the joint has finished cooking, pour over the port. Remove meat to a hot dish. Add the stock to the cooking liquor; skim off the fat; reheat and hand the gravy separately.

Serves 4–6

Braised Lamb with Stout

4 noisettes lamb   *8 button onions*
½ pint sweet stout   *1 teaspoon castor sugar*
2–3 ounces butter   *¼ pound mushrooms*
1 carrot (diced)

Melt the butter in a shallow saucepan and place the lamb, carrot, and onions in the pan. Sauté slowly for about ¼ hour, until the vegetables are browned, then remove them. Add sugar and sweet stout and simmer for ¼ hour. Peel, and fry mushrooms in a little butter and season. Mix cornflour with cold water to a paste and stir into the gravy. Add vegetables. Dish up noisettes, and garnish with mushrooms. Pour the sauce and vegetables round and serve with boiled new potatoes and green peas.

Serves 2

Curried Lamb

1½ pounds lamb (cooked)   *2 onions*
½ tablespoon curry powder *1 apple*
2 ounces butter   *⅛ pint light ale*

Cut meat into cubes. Peel and slice onion and sauté in butter in a shallow saucepan. Peel and slice apple. Add curry powder, apple, meat and beer to pan. Stir gently till the apple is soft. Place a circle of boiled rice round the curried meat. Serve with chutney of your choice.

Serves 4–6

Lamb Casserole

4 loin lamb chops
2 medium onions
4 large potatoes
1 ounce butter
¼ pint sweet stout

¼ pint stock (see p. 138)
2 tablespoons parsley (finely chopped)
seasoning to taste

Peel and slice potatoes and onions. Melt butter in a large frying pan and flame meat in it until browned on both sides. Add onions and sauté till soft. Arrange potato slices on the bottom of a well greased casserole dish and place onions and lamb on top. Add beer and stock; sprinkle with parsley and season. Cook covered in a moderate oven, 350°F, mark 4, for about 45 minutes or until meat is tender, basting from time to time.

Serves 4

Lamb Kebabs

1½ pounds lamb (raw)
¼ pint sweet stout
¼ pint pineapple juice (not syrup from tinned pineapple)
1 large green pepper

2 small onions
2 large tomatoes
1 clove garlic (crushed)
1 tablespoon soy sauce
2 tablespoons oil

First make a marinade of the beer, soy sauce, pineapple juice and garlic and soak lamb in this in the refrigerator overnight. Seed and thickly slice peppers; peel and slice onions and cut tomatoes into wedges. Drain lamb and spear on skewers, arranging alternately with sliced onion, pepper and tomato. Brush with oil and grill on a rôtisserie, or under the grill, turning frequently. Serve with savoury rice.

Serves 4

Stuffed Shoulder of Veal

3 pounds shoulder of veal   *1 clove garlic (crushed)*
½ pint light ale   *1 bay leaf*
10 anchovy fillets   *½ teaspoon thyme*
½ cup black olives (sliced)   *(powdered)*
1 cup breadcrumbs (white—   *2 tablespoons oil*
  see p. 137)   *seasoning to taste*

Have your butcher bone the veal and make a pocket to hold the stuffing. To make stuffing: mix together breadcrumbs, olives, anchovies and garlic. Stuff and tie securely. Place veal in a baking tin and brush with oil. Pour beer into bottom of tin and add bay leaf and thyme. Roast at 325°F, mark 3–4, for about 1½ hours or until meat is tender, basting with beer from time to time. Serve with boiled onions in white sauce and roast potatoes.

Serves 4

Breast of Veal in Beer

3 pounds breast of veal   *1 large onion (peeled and*
2 ounces butter   *sliced)*
pinch ground mace   *½ pint brown ale*
2 whole cloves   *seasoned flour (see p. 139)*

Have veal rolled, boned and tied securely with string by your butcher. Butter all over and roll in seasoned flour. Place on a rack in a roasting tin and bake in a hot oven, 450°F, mark 7–8, until lightly browned all over, turning as required. Remove rack. Add onion and herbs to the beer. Pour into tin and cover. Turn heat down to 325°F, mark 3, and cook until tender, allowing 25 minutes per pound. Dish up. Serve with braised celery and jacket potatoes and gravy in a hot sauce-boat.

Serves 4

Escalopes de Veau à la Bière

3 escalopes veal	2 tablespoons butter
¼ pint light ale	2 tablespoons double cream
1 cup Cheddar cheese	seasoned flour
(grated)	seasoning to taste
2 egg yolks	

Beat the veal escalopes with a cutlet bat to flatten. Dip in seasoned flour. Melt butter in a frying pan and sauté veal in this until cooked through and golden on both sides. Place in a serving dish and keep hot. Stir eggs into cream in a mixing bowl. Set aside. Pour beer into a saucepan and add grated cheese. Stir over a low flame until cheese is melted. Add eggs and cream gradually, stirring until sauce starts to thicken. Take great care not to boil up or overheat, as this would curdle the eggs. Pour sauce over veal and finish off by browning under grill. Serve with sauté potatoes and spinach.

Serves 3

Roast Loin of Veal

3 pounds loin of veal	1 tablespoon cornflour
(larded—see p. *139*)	2 ounces butter
3 medium carrots	1 bay leaf
3 medium onions	seasoning to taste
¼ pint brown ale	

Scrape and slice carrots; peel and thickly slice onions. Melt butter in a small saucepan. Place veal in a baking tin and surround with the sliced vegetables. Pour over melted butter and baste. Preheat oven to 400°F, mark 6, and bake meat and vegetables, turning frequently until browned. Add bay leaf to the vegetables and pour beer over the whole. Continue to cook for about 1 hour or until meat is tender, basting from time to time with the beer in the bottom of the baking tin. Mix cornflour with a little cold water to a paste. Dish up meat and vegetables and keep hot. Stir cornflour into liquid and meat juices left in baking tin and boil up, stirring continuously, until gravy is thick. Serve with new boiled potatoes and green peas.

Serves 4

Veal Chops Sauté à la Bière

4 veal chops	*1 bay leaf*
1 ounce butter	*1½ tablespoons flour*
2 medium onions	*seasoning to taste*
1 cup brown ale	

Season meat and melt butter in a large frying pan. Brown meat lightly on both sides. Peel and slice onion and add to veal; cook a few more minutes. Add beer and bay leaf and simmer until chops are tender. Mix flour with a little extra beer and stir smoothly into pan until sauce is slightly thickened. Serve with broccoli and sauté potatoes.

Serves 4

Ossi Bucchi

4 slices knuckle veal (cut into 3-inch lengths)	*3 tablespoons seasoned flour*
	1 tablespoon lemon juice
¼ pint brown ale	*3 tablespoons cooking oil*
¼ pint tomato purée	*½ cup white bone stock (see p. 138)*
1 head of celery	
3 large carrots	*1 teaspoon parsley (finely diced)*

Roll veal in seasoned flour and sauté in oil until well browned. Turn into a casserole. Trim and dice celery and scrape and dice carrots. Sauté in oil remaining in the frying pan. Add to casserole. Pour over beer, stock and tomato purée. Cover and cook in a moderate oven, 350°F, mark 4, for 1½–2 hours, or until tender. About 10 minutes before end of cooking time add parsley and lemon juice.

Serves 4

Liver with Beer

6 medium slices lamb's liver	¼ pint light ale
6 rashers back bacon	1 tablespoon cornflour
2 tablespoons cold water	

Remove any skin or piping from liver and sauté gently in butter with the bacon in a large frying pan. Remove bacon and liver and keep hot. Mix cornflour with cold water in a bowl till smooth and gradually add half the beer. Pour into pan and, stirring continuously, bring to the boil; gradually add remaining beer. Boil until reduced to required thickness and browning. Pour over liver and bacon and serve with creamed potatoes and braised cabbage.

Serves 3

Tripe in Ale

1¾ pounds tripe (cleaned and blanched)	4 medium onions
½ pint light ale	seasoning to taste

Prepare the dressed tripe by cutting it into pieces and layer into a casserole dish; pour over beer; season and cook in a moderate oven, 350°F, mark 4, for 2 hours. After 1 hour's cooking peel and halve the onions and add to the casserole. Serve with jacket potatoes.

Serves 4

Stewed Ox Tail

1 ox tail (average 2–2½ pounds)	½ pint stock
1 ounce seasoned flour	2 medium carrots (sliced thickly)
1½ ounces butter	bouquet garni (see p. 139)
2–3 ounces onion (sliced)	seasoning to taste
½ pint sweet stout	

Wash the ox tail, dry it and cut at each joint. Roll the pieces in seasoned flour and sauté in the butter until brown all over.

Remove to a casserole. Sauté in the remaining fat, blend in the
rest of the flour and continue frying for 2–3 minutes. Stir in
the stout and stock and bring to the boil stirring. Pour into
the casserole; add carrots, bouquet garni and seasoning. Cover
and simmer gently in the oven, 300°F, mark 2, for 2½–3½ hours, or
until the meat is really tender. Serve with piles of diced, glazed
vegetables of your choice.

Serves 4–5

Chicken Flemish Style

1 3-pound roasting chicken
1 quart light ale
2 ounces butter
3 large onions
1 tablespoon granulated
* sugar*
⅓ cup white vinegar
½ teaspoon prepared mustard
6 slices French bread
1 tablespoon mixed dry
* herbs*
seasoning to taste

Cut chicken and flame in butter in a frying pan. Peel and chop
onions. Sauté onions in pan with the chicken. Turn contents of
pan into a casserole dish. Add sugar and vinegar. Spread bread
with mustard and line around the sides of the casserole, mustard
side facing inward. Sprinkle herbs over casserole and cover with
beer. Season to taste; cover and cook over a low flame for about
1 hour or until chicken is tender. Serve with buttered egg
noodles instead of a vegetable.

Serves 4

Mexican Chicken with Rice

1 roasting chicken
½ cup oil
¾ pint light ale
2 medium onions (peeled and
* chopped)*
1 green pepper (chopped)
1 clove garlic (finely
* chopped)*
1 teaspoon paprika
1 8-ounce tin of tomato
* purée*
1 cup chicken stock (see p.
* 138)*
1 cup patna rice (raw)

Cut chicken into quarters and flame in oil in a frying pan. Add green pepper, onions and garlic and simmer for 25–30 minutes. Add rice and continue simmering until rice is cooked through.

Serves 4

Chicken and Beer Pilaf

1 3-pound chicken
8 ounces butter
2 ounces plain flour
½ teaspoon nutmeg (ground)
1 pint brown ale
1 tablespoon almonds (skinned and shredded— see p. 137)

½ pint cold water
3 cups rice (raw)
1 large onion (peeled and chopped)
seasoning to taste

Bone and cut chicken into several large pieces. Sauté in a large frying pan in half the butter until cooked through. Remove chicken and stir flour, nutmeg, seasoning and almonds into the fat left in the pan. Add water gradually and ½ pint of beer. Boil, stirring continuously, until this sauce reduces and thickens a little. Set aside. Melt remaining butter in a baking dish on top of the stove; add rice and chopped onion and stir until rice is about half cooked. Stir in remainder of beer; add sauce, chicken and enough water to well cover rice. Stir well and cook in a moderate oven, 350°F, mark 4, for ¾ hour. When cooked all the liquid should be absorbed by the rice. Serve hot.

Serves 4

Spring Chicken Stew

2 poussins
½ pint old ale
1 cup chicken stock (see p. 138)
2 sprigs parsley
1 blade mace

1 sprig thyme
1 stick celery
8 button onions
kneaded butter (see p. 139)
seasoning to taste

Split poussins in half and place in a large, shallow saucepan. Pour over beer and stock and add seasoning, thyme, parsley and

mace. Trim and chop celery and peel onions. Add to chicken
stew; cover and cook slowly until chicken is tender. Stir in
kneaded butter and bring to the boil, adding a little water if
gravy is becoming too thick. Cook for another 5 minutes, stirring
continuously. Serve with boiled potatoes and a green vegetable
of your choice.

Serves 4

Kent Fried Chicken

1 3-pound frying chicken   *seasoning to taste*
½ pint brown ale   *2 eggs*
1 cup oil   *2 cups breadcrumbs*
juice 1 lemon

Split the chicken into joints. Combine beer, lemon juice, half the
oil and seasoning to make a marinade. Steep chicken joints in
this marinade for at least 3 hours. Drain. Beat the eggs with a
little salt in a bowl and dip chicken joints in egg before coating
with crumbs. Take care to press breadcrumbs well in. Heat
remaining oil in a large frying pan and fry chicken joints gently
until tender, turning frequently. Serve with sauté potatoes, and
garnish with rashers of grilled streaky bacon and fried banana.

Serves 4

Italian Roast Chicken

1 3-pound roasting chicken   *2 tablespoons butter*
1 medium onion   *2 tablespoons tomato paste*
1 tablespoon mixed herbs   *juice 1 lemon*
  (dried)   *juice 1 orange*
2 cups breadcrumbs (fresh   *3 tablespoons oil*
  white—see p. 137)   *1 teaspoon brown sugar*
1 egg   *seasoning to taste*
½ pint light ale

First make the stuffing. Peel and finely chop the onion and mix
with breadcrumbs and herbs in a bowl. Soften with about 2

tablespoons of boiling water. Beat egg and mix into stuffing to bind. Stuff and truss chicken (*see* page 137). Pre-heat oven to 425°F, mark 5. Spread chicken with butter and place in a baking tin to roast for 20 minutes or until skin is crisp. Combine beer, tomato paste, fruit juices and oil and pour over chicken. Lower oven to 350°F, mark 4, and continue to roast for another hour or until chicken is tender, basting from time to time. Serve with château potatoes and broccoli.

Serves 4

Chicken Sauté Marengo

1 3-pound chicken	*2 teaspoons paprika*
2 ounces butter	*¼ pint single cream*
6 small onions	*1 bay leaf*
½ pint brown ale	*seasoning to taste*
3 tablespoons tomato purée	

First joint the chicken. Melt the butter in a flameproof casserole and brown chicken joints in it. Peel onions and add whole. Cook over a medium flame until onions soften. Season and sprinkle with paprika. Stir in tomato purée and beer and add the bay leaf. Cover with a lid and continue to simmer for about ¾ hour or until chicken is tender. Remove bay leaf. Skim fat and stir in cream. Leave to simmer for a few minutes to let cream heat through. Serve with boiled rice or sauté potatoes.

Serves 4

Duck Casserole with Rice

1 5–6-pound duck	*¼ pint brown ale*
2 tablespoons oil	*¾ pint water*
2 cloves garlic (crushed)	*1½ cups rice (raw)*
2 teaspoons paprika	*1 cup fresh peas (cooked)*

Cut duck into small pieces, removing as much fat as you can. Heat the oil in a flameproof casserole dish and add the garlic.

Brown duck pieces on all sides. Pour off excess fat. Season and sprinkle with paprika. Bring ¼ pint of water to the boil and pour over. Simmer for ¾ hour before adding remaining boiling water. Mix in rice and continue to cook for 20 minutes. Add peas and cook until rice is tender. Mix in beer, season and simmer for a final 5 minutes.

Serves 4–5

Ragoût of Duck

1 4–5-pound duck
seasoned flour
¼ pint brown ale
¾ pint white bone stock
  (see p. 138)

2 shallots
bouquet garni
2 ounces butter
1 tablespoon flour
seasoning to taste

Divide duck into 4 pieces. Dip in seasoned flour and set aside. Melt butter in a shallow saucepan and fry duck pieces until brown on all sides. Peel shallots and add to duck with stock, brown ale and bouquet garni. Cover and stew slowly for about ¾ hour or until meat is tender. Mix flour with cold water to a paste. Remove bouquet garni and skim fat from gravy. Thicken gravy by stirring in flour and water paste and boiling up. Place pieces of duck on a serving dish and pour gravy over. Serve with croûtes of fried bread, game chips and peas.

Serves 4

Salmis of Duckling

1 duckling
2 ounces butter
2 medium onions
¼ pint chicken stock
  (see p. 138)

½ pint light ale
pinch thyme
pinch Basil
2 tablespoons flour

Joint the duck as for a chicken and remove as much fat as you can. Melt butter in a casserole. Peel and chop onions. Sauté pieces of duck in the butter until browned on all sides. Pour off excess fat and add onion, flour, beer, stock and herbs. Cover and bring to the boil. Simmer for about 1 hour or until duck is tender. Skim off excess fat before serving. Serve with lattice crisps, green peas and new boiled potatoes.

Serves 4

Orange Sauce

3 tablespoons orange rind (grated)	*½ cup chicken consommé*
	¼ pint light ale
1 tablespoon cornflour	*1 tablespoon brown sugar*
1 cup orange juice	*½ teaspoon salt*

Pour boiling water over orange rind and let soak for 10 minutes, then drain. Mix cornflour with a little orange juice until smooth. Combine in a saucepan with remaining orange juice, consommé, light ale, brown sugar and salt. Cook over low heat, stirring constantly to boiling. Add rind and cook for another 10 minutes. Serve with game or duck.

Partridge Casserole

3 French partridges	*bouquet garni*
¼ pint brown ale	*1½ cups breadcrumbs*
½ pint stock (see below)	*1 cup raisins*
1 medium onion	*½ cup walnuts (chopped)*
1 large carrot	*1 sprig parsley (chopped)*
2 rashers streaky bacon	*1 egg (beaten)*
4 chipolata sausages	*seasoning to taste*
1 dessertspoon flour	*croûtes fried bread*

First of all bone out the partridges as you would a chicken but leaving in the leg bones. Make stock from the carcasses, a selection of root vegetables and bouquet garni as for brown bone stock (*see* page 138). Strain ½ pint and set aside. Make stuffing for the partridges by mixing breadcrumbs, raisins, walnuts, seasoning and parsley together; chop and lightly cook shallot in 1 ounce of butter and add to stuffing. Bind stuffing mixture with beaten egg. Lay partridges flat and spread with stuffing. Sew up securely with fine string using a trussing needle. Peel and slice onion and carrot and dice bacon rashers. In a large casserole brown sausages in remaining butter. Remove and brown partridges. Add onion, carrot and bacon and, after 5 minutes' cooking, dust with flour and add beer, stock and bouquet garni.

Pre-heat oven to 325°F, mark 3, and cook partridge casserole for about 1 hour or until birds are tender. Remove birds from casserole and return sausages to it to re-heat for a few minutes. Serve partridges, split in half, on croûtes of fried bread, garnished with sausage halves and a little of the sauce. Serve with bread sauce and game chips and remaining sauce separately.

Serves 4–5

Stuffed Pheasant

1 large pheasant (or 2 hens)	*1 tablespoon arrowroot*
4 ounces butter	*6 ounces ham (cooked and*
½ pint light ale	*shredded)*
bouquet garni	*1 cup breadcrumbs (fresh*
¼ pint stock	*white—see p. 137)*
3 cooking apples	*1 teaspoon mixed herbs*
1 tablespoon brown sugar	*(dried)*
3 tablespoons double cream	*1 egg (beaten)*

First make the stuffing. Mix breadcrumbs, herbs and ham together. Peel and chop onion and sauté until soft in about 1 ounce of butter. Add the onion and butter in which it was cooked to the stuffing. Bind stuffing with beaten egg. Bone out the pheasant as for chicken leaving leg bones in and fill with stuffing. Sew pheasant up with a trussing needle and fine string so that it regains its usual shape. Heat remaining butter in a flameproof casserole and brown pheasant all round. Add stock, about $\frac{1}{4}$ pint of the light ale and bouquet garni. Cover and cook in a moderate oven at 350°F, mark 4, for about $\frac{3}{4}$ hour or until bird is tender. Meanwhile, prepare beer and apple sauce. Core but do not peel apples. Cook to a pulp with remaining butter and rub through a strainer. Return to pan and add remaining beer, seasoning and sugar. Simmer for a few minutes. Remove the pheasant from casserole, carve and keep hot on a serving dish. Add strained liquid from casserole to apple sauce. Mix arrowroot with a little cold water and stir into the sauce to thicken. Add cream. Leave to simmer for a few seconds before pouring some of the sauce over the pheasant. Serve remaining sauce separately. Serve stuffed pheasant with braised celery and château potatoes.

Serves 4

Marinated Venison

3 pounds venison (cut into large chunks)	pinch thyme
	pinch Oregano
1 pint light ale	1 bay leaf
2 tablespoons vinegar	seasoning to taste
1 large onion	oil for cooking
2 cloves garlic (crushed)	1 tablespoon cornflour
6 large tomatoes	

First make a marinade of the beer, vinegar, garlic, seasoning and herbs. Peel and finely chop the onion and add to the marinade. Steep venison in this in the refrigerator overnight. Drain meat and set marinade aside. Brown the meat in the oil in a flame-proof casserole dish. Meanwhile, scald and skin tomatoes. Add tomatoes and marinade to casserole; cover and cook slowly over a low flame until tender. Mix cornflour to a paste with a little cold water and stir into gravy to thicken. Serve with braised celery, glazed carrots and new boiled potatoes.

Serves 4

Venison Chasseur

4 medallions venison	juice 1 lemon
2 ounces butter	1 tablespoon sour cream
½ cup oil	4 mushrooms (large flat)
½ pint light ale	watercress to garnish
4 croûtes fried bread	
1 tablespoon redcurrant jelly	

Have the butcher cut 4 round medallions about ½ inch thick from a saddle of venison. Melt butter and oil in a frying pan and quickly brown venison on one side; turn and cook on other side to required rareness. Remove from pan and keep hot. Peel and sauté whole mushrooms, in a little butter in a separate pan. Meanwhile, pour off most of butter and oil from frying pan and deglaze with beer. Boil up; season and stir in redcurrant jelly and lemon juice. Slowly stir in cream. Arrange croûtes of fried bread on a serving dish with a venison medallion on each one and a mushroom on top. Garnish with watercress. Serve hot gravy separately in a sauce boat. Serve with sauté potatoes and braised leeks.

Serves 4

Jugged Hare

1 hare (with the blood)	20 pickling onions
2 ounces butter	1 large onion (sliced)
1 ounce flour	3 tablespoons oil
1 pint sweet stout	2 sprigs parsley
1 pint brown bone stock (see p. 138)	1 bay leaf
	1 sprig thyme
4 rashers streaky bacon	2 tablespoons brandy
¼ pound button mushrooms	croûtes fried bread

Joint the hare, cutting the back into pieces. Set aside the blood. Make a marinade of the oil, parsley, bay leaf, thyme, onion

slices and brandy and steep hare in this in the refrigerator overnight. Remove and drain. Chop bacon into small strips and
brown in the butter in a flameproof casserole. Remove bacon
and add pickling onions to cook until soft. Set aside with bacon.
Blend the flour with the fat remaining in the casserole and cook
pieces of hare until browned on all sides. Add the beer and stock
gradually, stirring continuously and bring to the boil. Cover
casserole and cook in a low oven, 325°F, mark 3, for $1\frac{1}{2}$ hours.
At the end of this time, strain sauce and return to casserole with
the mushrooms and bacon and cook for a further $\frac{1}{4}$ hour. Thicken
sauce with blood just before serving with triangular croûtes of
fried bread and new boiled potatoes.

Serves 4

Fish and Shellfish

YOU WILL find white fish, shellfish or oily fish—whichever is your favourite—more exciting cooked in beer. Fish and chips takes on a new meaning when you fry the fish in light, aromatic beer batter, and a beer sauce will turn any plain fried, grilled or boiled fish into a gourmet dish.

Fish is as much a part of our daily life as beer itself and the varieties of delicious fish to be found in our seas and rivers is unsurpassed anywhere in the world. However, we do have a tendency in Britain to be unadventurous in our choice of fish. Try some of the more unusual ones in this chapter such as bass, carp, eel or mackerel for a change and see how superb they can be.

When frying fish in batter make sure that the fat is heated to the required temperature before dropping in the coated fish so that the batter will crisp and swell immediately. Never crowd the pan; leave plenty of room to turn fish, frying in several batches if necessary and removing any scraps of batter which may be left in the pan between batches. Drain fish on absorbent paper before serving.

To grill white fish such as sole, plaice or whiting, have it skinned by your fishmonger first and in some cases filleted as well. Leave the head on to grill, brush first with melted butter and turn after a few minutes.

As well as fish in beer batters and beer sauces, you will find that fish actually cooked in beer acquires a subtly different flavour and appetising aroma. Shellfish, in particular, lends itself to this method for the beer enhances its natural flavours.

Beer Sauce for Fish

1 pint lager	*1 bay leaf*
1 teaspoon vinegar	*½ ounce butter*
1 teaspoon brown sugar	*¼ teaspoon cinnamon*
1 medium onion	*seasoning to taste*
1 clove garlic	*2 tablespoons cornflour*

Place all the ingredients except the cornflour in a large saucepan and bring to the boil. Simmer for 15 minutes. Strain. Mix cornflour with a little cold water to a paste. Stir into sauce and return to heat, stirring continuously until sauce thickens. Delicious over white fish such as baked haddock or steamed cod.

Whiting Dijonnaise

4 whiting	*butter*
½ pint brown ale	*8 hard-boiled eggs*
8 ounces Cheddar cheese (grated)	*4 tomatoes*
2 level teaspoons dijon mustard (made)	

First, grill the fish in butter, and put into an ovenproof dish. Scald, skin and slice tomatoes and slice eggs. Make a sauce by melting a knob of butter in a pan, adding the grated cheese, mustard and the ale. Stir until the cheese melts. Pour over the fish, and brown under the grill.

Serves 4

Braised Salmon

2 thick salmon steaks	*2 ounces butter*
½ pint pale ale	*seasoning*
2 sticks celery	*lemon slices and parsley to garnish*
4 shallots	
2 young carrots	

Trim and slice celery and place in a shallow saucepan. Peel and slice carrots and shallots and add to pan with butter and ale. Season to taste. Cover and cook slowly for about 15 minutes. Place steaks side by side in a shallow casserole dish. Pour over sauce and cover. Cook in a low oven, 325°F, mark 3, until salmon is tender. Dish up. Pour the sauce into a saucepan and bring to the boil. Boil, stirring constantly, until a creamy consistency and pour over fish. Garnish with sprigs of parsley and slices of lemon.

Serves 2–4

Dover Sole au Gratin

1 Dover Sole	*½ pint brown ale*
seasoning to taste	*1 tablespoon flour*
2 ounces butter	*½ cup breadcrumbs (browned*
3 chives (chopped)	*—see p. 137)*
1 small onion (peeled and	*½ cup Cheddar cheese*
diced)	*(grated)*

Wipe sole clean. Brush with lemon juice and season. Place in a buttered casserole dish. Sprinkle with chives and onion. Add ¼ pint brown ale. Bake in a moderate oven, 350°F, mark 4, for about 15 minutes, until the flesh is looking creamy. Drain off beer stock. Melt ½ ounce butter in a saucepan and stir in flour. When the mixture turns a pale brown, gradually stir in the beer stock and another ¼ pint of ale. Bring to the boil, stirring constantly. Strain over sole. Sprinkle with breadcrumbs and grated cheese and brown under grill. Serve with new boiled, or creamed, potatoes.

Serves 2

Baked Fillet of Sole

2 pounds lemon sole (fillets)	*1 ounce butter*
½ pint light ale	*1 tablespoon flour*
1 onion (chopped)	*½ cup sour cream*
¼ teaspoon ginger	*paprika*
½ teaspoon caraway seeds	

Well butter a baking dish and lay fillets in it with onion, ginger and caraway seeds. Pour over three-quarters of the ale. Season and bake for about 20 minutes at 325°F, mark 3. Melt butter in a saucepan. Blend in flour until golden. Pour liquid from baking dish into a cup and add remaining ale gradually. Add to flour mixture, stirring continuously until smooth and thickened. Add sour cream and pour sauce over fillets. Sprinkle with paprika and brown under grill. Serve with a border of creamed potatoes.

Serves 4

Sole in Ginger Sauce

4 fillets sole	¼ pint chicken broth
2 tablespoons lager	2 tablespoons vinegar
5 tablespoons corn starch	2 tablespoons sugar
salt to taste	1 tablespoon tomato ketchup
½ cup breadcrumbs (fine)	1 tablespoon ginger
3 tablespoons water	(powdered)
3 tablespoons oil	fat for deep frying

Wash and dry sole fillets and cut in half. Mix the lager, 4 tablespoons corn starch, egg yolks and salt together and dip fish in this mixture. Coat with crumbs, taking care to press the crumbs well in. Heat fat in a deep fryer to 365°F and fry fillets until cooked through and browned. Meanwhile, mix last tablespoon of corn starch with cold water, in a saucepan. Stir in broth, oil, vinegar, sugar, ketchup and ginger. Simmer, stirring continuously until sauce thickens. Dish up sole and pour sauce over. Serve with petits pois.

Serves 4

Casserole of Sole

4 fillets sole	6 eggs (hard-boiled and
½ pint brown ale	sliced)
½ pound Cheddar cheese	4 tomatoes (skinned and
(grated)	sliced)
2 teaspoons English mustard	2 ounces butter
(made)	

Grill the sole in some of the butter. Lay in a casserole dish and cover with sliced eggs and sliced tomatoes. Make a sauce by heating remaining butter in a saucepan and stirring in grated cheese, beer and mustard. When cheese is melted pour sauce over fish casserole. Brown top under the grill.

Serves 4

Beer Baked Plaice

2 plaice (filleted)	1 bay leaf
3 ounces butter	$\frac{1}{4}$ pound mushrooms
$\frac{1}{4}$ cup breadcrumbs (browned)	2 shallots (chopped)
1 large potato	1 tablespoon parsley (finely
$\frac{1}{4}$ pint light ale	chopped)
$\frac{1}{4}$ pint water	1 tablespoon flour
6 peppercorns	5 fluid ounces single cream

Wash, dry and skin fillets of plaice and lay, folded in two, in a well-buttered flameproof dish. Pour over ale and water. Add bay leaf and seasoning. Peel and roughly grate potato. Soak in cold water for 15 minutes. Dry and fry in 1 ounce butter; separating flakes from each other with a fork. When crisp take out and keep warm. Pre-heat oven to 350°F, mark 4, and cook plaice in beer for 10 minutes to $\frac{1}{4}$ hour. Meanwhile, fry shallots and mush-rooms in another 1 ounce butter until soft. Season and add parsley. Blend remaining butter and flour in a pan and gradually add liquid from plaice casserole. Stir continuously until sauce thickens. Add cream and leave to simmer for a couple of minutes. Arrange mushrooms and shallots on a serving dish, lay plaice fillets on top and coat with sauce, crumbs and potato.

Serves 4

Maiden's Proving

This recipe was the old-fashioned way of testing the worth of an intended bride—if the fish were stuffed so full that it burst she would be an improvident wife; if it were not full enough she

would be tight-fisted but if it were just right the lucky bride-
groom would immediately rush off to arrange the wedding!

1 mackerel	*flour to bind*
2 shallots (chopped)	*black pepper (fresh ground)*
2 ounces butter	*¼ pint brown ale*
2 tablespoons breadcrumbs	*2 tablespoons lemon juice*
1 teaspoon mixed herbs	*seasoning to taste*

Make a stuffing by mixing breadcrumbs, herbs, flour, black
pepper and butter together with a little boiling water. Trim head
and tail from fish, clean and make a slit down one side. Stuff fish.
Lay fish in a well-greased casserole dish; dot with butter and
sprinkle chopped shallots on top. Pour beer over and cook,
covered, in a moderate oven, 325°F, mark 3, for about 20
minutes or until cooked through. Carefully remove fish. Mix
flour to a paste with a little cold water and stir into sauce to
thicken. Add lemon juice. Pour sauce over fish and serve with
potatoes of your choice.

Serves 2

Halibut in Lager

2 medium halibut steaks	*4 large tomatoes*
2 ounces butter	*seasoning to taste*
2 tablespoons lager	*parsley to garnish (finely*
seasoned flour	*chopped)*

Wipe the fish steaks and dip in seasoned flour. Melt the butter in
the bottom of a grill and lay fish in it skin side down, spooning
butter over. Grill this side under a hot grill for a few minutes
then pour lager over and continue to grill until this side is cooked.
Turn fish and grill second side under a lower heat. Meanwhile,
scald and skin tomatoes and slice thinly. Dish up fish with a layer
of tomatoes on top sprinkled with parsley and a little of the sauce
from the grill pan spooned over.

Serves 2

Skate au Gratin

1½ pounds skate	1 bay leaf
1 teaspoon flour	½ pint light ale
seasoning to taste	1 cup Cheddar cheese
2 spring onions	(grated)
pinch of thyme (powdered)	12 shallots (boiled)

Skin skate and place in a fish kettle. Sprinkle with the flour and seasoning. Finely chop spring onions and add with bay leaf, thyme and beer. Bring to boiling point then simmer for 20 minutes. Strain off the liquid. Butter a shallow casserole dish and cover with the cheese. Place skate on top. Arrange shallots round it. Pour over stock and cover with more cheese. Brown under grill until cheese is melted and turned golden.

Serves 3

Trout in Beer

2 trout	½ cup vinegar
1 cup light ale	4 slices lemon
1 cup dry white wine	parsley to serve

Clean and prepare trout and place in a shallow saucepan. Mix beer, vinegar and white wine together and pour over fish. Bring to the boil and simmer till cooked. Drain and garnish with lemon slices and parsley. Serve with new potatoes.

Serves 2

Fillets of Trout in Beer

2 pounds trout fillets	1 tablespoon brown sugar
2 cups sweet stout	1 tablespoon lemon juice
2 ounces butter	6 black peppercorns
2 tablespoons flour	1 clove
½ teaspoon salt	

Melt the butter in a shallow saucepan and stir in the flour. Gradually stir in the beer and cook, stirring constantly, till sauce thickens. Add peppercorns, clove, salt and sugar. Add the trout fillets face down. Cover and simmer for 10–15 minutes, turning fillets after 5 minutes. When cooked remove and keep hot. Add lemon juice to the sauce and strain over the fish.

Serves 6

Baked Herrings

6 herrings	1 onion (peeled, medium sized)
1 teaspoon ground allspice	3 bay leaves
6 whole cloves	salt to taste
1 teaspoon black pepper	¼ pint vinegar
(fresh ground)	¼ pint light ale

Clean, wash and dry herrings but leave whole. Season with allspice. Place side by side in a shallow baking dish. Add the cloves and pepper. Peel and slice onion and arrange slices on top of fish with the bay leaves. Mix vinegar and beer together and pour over the fish. Cover with greased paper and bake in a slow oven, 300°F, mark 2, for about 1¼ hours. Remove paper and baste with the liquid. Leave for a couple of hours to get cold. Serve with salad of your choice.

Serves 4–6

Soused Herrings

4 large herrings	seasoned flour
¼ pint lager	2 ounces butter
2 Spanish onions (sliced)	chives to garnish
2 tablespoons vinegar	

Cut heads and tails off herrings. Clean, split and open out flat, removing backbone. Coat in seasoned flour. Heat butter in a frying pan and gently fry herrings until just cooked but not falling apart. Carefully remove herrings to a shallow serving plate. Leave to cool for 15 minutes. Cover herrings with slices of onion. Mix lager and vinegar together and pour over herrings and onions. Leave to chill and absorb dressing in the refrigerator for at least 4 hours before serving. Garnish with snipped chives.

Serves 4

Beer Batter for Fish (1)

1 cup flour
⅛ pint light ale

¼ teaspoon pepper
½ teaspoon salt

Blend all ingredients together. Dip fish into batter and fry in hot oil or fat.

Beer Batter for Fish (2)

2 eggs (separated—see
  p. 137)
¼ pint light ale
1 cup flour
¾ teaspoon salt

1 ounce butter (melted)
1½ pounds white fish fillets of
  your choice
fat for frying

Beat beer and egg yolks together and stir in flour and salt until thoroughly mixed. Mix in butter and leave to stand for about ½ hour. Beat egg whites until stiff and fold into mixture. Heat fat in a deep fryer to 365°F. Dip fish pieces into batter and drop into pre-heated fat. Cook until lightly browned. Drain before serving.

Serves 4–6

Cod Fries

1 pound cod
¼–½ pint light ale
2½ cups plain flour
1 teaspoon baking powder
1 clove garlic (finely
  chopped)

4 shallots (finely chopped)
2 tablespoons parsley
  (chopped)
Fat for deep frying

Soak cod. Lightly poach, remove skin and shred fish. Sift flour and baking powder together in a large bowl. Mix in garlic, shallots, parsley and black pepper. Add enough beer to make a batter consistency and add cod. Heat fat in a deep fryer to 380°F.

Drop batter by spoonfuls into hot fat and fry until brown. Drain and serve hot.

Serves 3

Eels in Beer (1)

$1\frac{1}{2}$ pound eel
1 medium onion
1 pint light ale
1 ounce butter
1 teaspoon chopped parsley
  or chives

squeeze lemon juice
1 tablespoon flour
seasoning to taste

Wash and skin eel. Cut into inch-thick steaks. Peel and chop onion. Pour beer into a large saucepan and add onion, seasoning, butter and eel steaks. Simmer gently until eel is tender. Arrange eels on a hot serving dish. Strain liquid and return to saucepan. Mix flour with a little water to a paste and add to liquid, stirring all the time to thicken, and pour over eel steaks. Garnish with parsley.

Serves 4

Eels in Beer (2)

1 pound eel steaks
seasoning to taste
1 tablespoon flour
3 ounces butter
1 tablespoon minced onion
$\frac{1}{4}$ pound peeled mushrooms

$\frac{1}{2}$ pint brown ale
1 teaspoon minced parsley
  or chives
$\frac{1}{2}$ gill cream
$\frac{1}{2}$ teaspoon lemon juice

Season eel steaks and dip in flour. Peel and slice mushrooms and onions and sauté in butter with eel steaks, turning them from time to time. Add beer. Simmer very gently until tender. Add parsley or chives, then remainder of butter, bit by bit. Slowly stir in the cream, and seasoning to taste then lemon juice. Serve with new potatoes.

Serves 2

Spiced Carp in Beer

1 carp, with roe	6 black peppercorns
2 ounces butter	½ teaspoon celery salt
1 large onion	1 whole clove
1 sprig parsley	seasoning to taste
1 sprig thyme	brown ale as required

Remove roe from carp and set aside. Poach carp gently in salted water with a dash of lemon juice. Fillet carefully, leaving half the head attached to each fillet and removing bitter sac from head. Melt butter and sauté onion in it until tender. Place in the bottom of a fish kettle. Add the bay leaf, parsley, thyme, peppercorns, clover and celery salt. Season fillets on both sides and lay on top of onions side by side. Add enough brown ale to cover. Simmer gently for 25 minutes. When cooked, drain and arrange on a dish. Re-heat sauce, stirring constantly, then add a pat of butter and pour over fish. Slice roe. Arrange round fish alternately with sprigs of parsley.

Serves 2–3

Carp Braised in Beer

2 pounds carp steaks	2 tablespoons flour
seasoning to taste	2 bay leaves
1 stick celery	½ pint brown ale
6 spring onions	2 ounces butter
1 tablespoon nutmeg (grated)	

Peel and chop onions and trim and dice celery. Place in the bottom of a large casserole dish and lay carp steaks on top. Season and sprinkle nutmeg over. Add bay leaves and beer. Cover. Bring to boil on top of the stove, then place in a slow oven, 300°F, mark 2, for about 15 minutes until cooked. Dish up carp and keep hot. Mix flour with a little water and stir into liquid over heat to thicken. Strain into a saucepan and add butter. Bring to the boil and pour over fish.

Serves 4

Carp with Gingerbread

A traditional German dish usually served at Christmas.

1 medium carp, with roe	*1 teaspoon ground cinnamon*
3 carrots	*2 tablespoons vinegar*
1 medium onion	*1 teaspoon treacle*
1 bay leaf	*1½ ounces gingerbread*
juice and rind 1 lemon	*3 tablespoons butter*
½ pint brown ale	*1 tablespoon flour*

Scale and clean the carp and set aside the roe. Place in a fish kettle. Peel and slice onion and carrots. Grate lemon rind and add to the fish with the lemon juice, bay leaf, cinnamon, gingerbread (crumbled) vinegar and beer. Bring to the boil and allow to boil for about 10 minutes, then simmer for another 10–15 minutes until fish is cooked. Meanwhile, prepare croûtes and lightly poach roe in a little salted water and lemon juice. Sauté mushrooms and chop parsley. Dish up fish on croûtes on a serving dish and garnish with mushrooms, roe and parsley. Thicken remaining stock by mixing flour with a little cold water and stirring into liquid over heat. Coat fish with a little of this and serve remaining sauce separately.

Serves 2

Bass Boiled in Beer

3 pounds bass	*1 tablespoon brown sugar*
¼ pound butter	*6 black peppercorns*
2 medium onions	*pinch ground cloves*
2 tablespoons flour	*1 tablespoon vinegar*
¾ pint brown ale	

Clean, scale and rinse fish and cut into slices. Melt the butter in a saucepan and stir in flour. Add beer, sugar, peppercorns, and cloves and stir till boiling. Add the fish slices. Simmer gently for another couple of minutes. Dish up with a little of the sauce over the fish and the remainder served separately. Serve with creamed potatoes.

Serves 6

Shrimps in Beer

2 pounds shrimps (raw)   ¼ teaspoon thyme
½ pint light ale   2 red peppers (dried)
2 bay leaves

Place shrimps in a saucepan with the beer and bay leaves and
bring to the boil. Add peppers and herbs and simmer for 5
minutes with a lid on. Cool shrimps in the liquid. Remove
shrimps from liquid when cold. Shell, de-vein and chill in the
refrigerator before serving. Serve with a salad of your choice.

Serves 6

Prawns in Beer

3 pounds prawns   3 sprigs fresh dill
½ pint light ale   fresh celery leaves
1 bay leaf   12 peppercorns

Wash prawns and place in a saucepan with the beer. Bring to the
boil. Add remaining ingredients and simmer for 5 minutes. Leave
prawns to cool in the liquid and when cold drain, shell, de-vein
and serve with a salad of your choice.

Serves 8

Stuffed Prawns

1 pound prawns (shelled and   ⅓ cup light ale
  de-veined)   2 tablespoons parsley (finely
¼ pound cream cheese   chopped)
2 ounces Danish blue cheese

Cook prawns in boiling, salted water for 10 minutes. Drain and
allow to get really cold. Mix cheese together with a little of the
beer, gradually adding all of it. Slit prawns partway along vein
side and stuff with the cheese mixture. Roll cheese side in parsley
and serve as party appetisers.

Lobster in Beer Sauce

2 large lobsters (live)   3 shallots (peeled and diced)
court bouillon   1 tablespoon cornflour
1 pint light ale   a little cold water
6 caraway seeds   watercress to garnish
3 black peppercorns

Cook the lobsters in the court bouillon for ½ hour. Meanwhile, pour beer into a saucepan with the spices and peeled and diced shallots. Bring to the boil slowly. Mix cornflour in a bowl with a little cold water and add to saucepan, stirring all the time to thicken. Dish up lobsters, split in half with the sauce poured over. Garnish with watercress.

Serves 2

Fruits de Mer à la Bière

1 dozen oysters   1 medium onion
¼ pint prawns (boiled)   4 shallots (peeled)
¼ pint crab meat (flaked and   1 bay leaf
  cooked)   1 sprig parsley
2 ounces butter   1 stick celery
1 tablespoon flour   seasoning to taste
1 pint light ale

Peel and slice onion and shallots and trim and slice celery. Pour beer into a saucepan and add vegetables, bay leaf, parsley and seasoning. Bring to boiling point. Simmer gently for about 15 minutes then add seasoning to taste. Shell oysters and keep in their liquor for 3–5 minutes until they plump out and the edges begin to curl. Drain. Add to beer with the prawns and crab meat. Knead the butter and flour into a paste and stir into sauce. Remove bay leaf and parsley and stir till boiling. Serve with plain boiled rice.

Serves 4

Hungarian Scallops

1 pound scallops
1 pint lager
¾ tablespoon butter
¾ tablespoon flour
½ cup thick cream

1 dessertspoon parsley
(chopped)
¼ teaspoon paprika
1 bay leaf

Prepare and wash scallops. Place in a saucepan and cover with beer. Bring to the boil and add bay leaf. Cover and simmer for about 5 minutes. Remove scallops and quarter. Continue to boil beer till reduced to half its quantity. Melt the butter in a small saucepan and stir in the flour. Add the beer. Simmer for a few minutes before stirring in cream and parsley off the heat. Return pan to stove, add paprika and scallops. Draw pan to side of stove Cover and leave for a few minutes for scallops to re-heat.

Serves 4

Mixed Seafood with Rice

½ pound raw prawns
½ pound raw lobster meat
½ pound scallops (chopped)
1 pint brown ale
pinch salt
2 sprigs parsley
2 thin slices lemon
1 bay leaf

6 black peppercorns
3 shallots (chopped)
2 ounces butter
2 tablespoons flour
½ cup tomato sauce
salt and cayenne pepper to
to taste
pinch of sugar

Pour beer into a saucepan and add salt, parsley, lemon, bay leaf, peppercorns, and shallots. Bring to the boil and add shellfish. Simmer for a few minutes. Meanwhile, melt butter and stir in flour. When blended, and the fish is cooked, remove fish to a plate and gradually strain the beer into the roux off the heat. When mixed, cook, stirring constantly, till smooth and thick, then stir in tomato sauce. Simmer for 10 minutes, stirring constantly, then add shellfish, seasoning to taste, and sugar. Stir till hot. Serve on a bed of boiled rice.

Serves 6

Seafood Salad

6 ounces prawns (shelled)	1 clove garlic (crushed)
6 ounces crab meat (flaked)	4 eggs (hard-boiled)
1 quart fresh mussels (cooked and shelled)	½ cup oil
	⅛ pint light ale
2 small beetroots (cooked)	2 tablespoons vinegar
3 new potatoes (boiled)	seasoning to taste
½ cucumber (peeled and diced)	6 prawns (with heads on) to garnish
2 tablespoons green peas (cooked)	watercress to garnish

Mix all the fish, except the prawns for garnishing, together in a large bowl with the vegetables. Make a dressing by combining oil, beer, vinegar, garlic and seasoning and toss seafood in this, reserving a little of the dressing. Arrange seafood on a serving dish. Peel and slice hard-boiled eggs and place around edges of dish. Garnish with watercress and whole prawns and pour over remaining dressing. Serve cold as a summer luncheon dish.

Serves 4

Vegetables and Salads

WHETHER YOU want an unusual vegetable to go with a particular dish or a classic vegetable main course, such as a *cassoulet* or *choucroûte*, you will find that cooking vegetables in beer makes a world of difference to their taste and fresh appearance.

In this chapter you will find a large selection of vegetables and vegetable dishes cooked in beer, together with a variety of salads. As well as making the recipes given here, use the beer batters to coat your favourite vegetables and see how delicious the result is; or experiment with the salad dressings on your own choice of salad.

Even the dullest old boiled cabbage, with its overtones of school dinners and boarding house kitchens, can be turned into a mouthwatering delicacy if it is carefully braised in beer.

Beer Batter for Vegetables

1½ cups plain flour   *2 tablespoons lard*
1 cup light ale   *1 egg (lightly beaten)*
1 teaspoon salt

Sift flour and salt in a mixing bowl. Cut lard into small pieces and rub in until mixture resembles fine crumbs. Mix in egg and light ale and beat until smooth. Makes a delicious batter for potatoes (*see* page 71), cauliflower, aubergines or asparagus.

Makes 2 cups batter

Potato Fritters

2 pounds potato (mashed)   ½ teaspoon baking powder
5 egg yolks   ½ pint brown ale
4 tablespoons butter (melted)   2 tablespoons salad oil
1½ teaspoons salt   1 egg white (stiffly beaten)
¼ teaspoon pepper   oil or fat for deep frying
8 ounces flour (sifted)

Beat up potato with 4 egg yolks, butter, salt and pepper and shape
into 1-inch balls; chill. Make batter by mixing together flour,
baking powder, brown ale and oil and remaining egg yolk and
folding in egg white. Heat oil or fat to 375° and drop in potato
balls dipped in batter (do not crowd them) and drain while preparing remainder.

Makes 30 fritters

Beer-Batter Onions

6 ounces flour (sifted)   ¼ pint lager
1 teaspoon salt   2 tablespoons salad oil
pinch pepper   3–4 large Spanish onions
2 eggs (separated—   oil or fat for frying
  see p. 137)

Sift flour, salt and pepper into a bowl. Whisk egg yolks, lager and
oil and add to flour mixture, stirring only until smooth; let stand
for one hour. Slice onions into rings not more than ¼-inch thick
and separate into rings. Beat egg whites until stiff but not dry and
fold into the batter. Dip onion rings, coating them thoroughly,
and fry on both sides in oil or fat about 2 inches deep and heated to
about 365°F until browned on both sides. Drain and keep hot
while preparing remainder.

Serves 6

Braised Amsterdam Cabbage

4 pounds cabbage
3 tablespoons butter
1 teaspoon salt
¼ teaspoon black pepper
  (fresh ground)

½ teaspoon sugar
1 tablespoon flour
½ pint light ale

Shred cabbage coarsely and sauté for five minutes in the butter, stirring frequently. Sprinkle with the salt, pepper, sugar and flour, mixing lightly. Add the light ale, cover and cook for 10 minutes over low heat.

Serves 6

Beer Potatoes

2 pounds small potatoes
beer batter (see p. 69)

fat for deep frying

Peel and halve potatoes. Dip in batter, coating completely and fry in a deep fat bath or chip pan at 365°F, for about 10 minutes, or until golden. Drain.

Serves 4

Asparagus Parmesan

1 pound fresh asparagus
2 ounces butter (melted)
½ pint light ale

½ teaspoon salt
½ teaspoon black pepper
  (fresh ground)

Wash and trim asparagus and cook until tender in boiling salted water. Drain and place in a shallow casserole dish. Pour beer round and season. Cover and cook in the oven at 435°F, mark 7, for about ¼ hour. Asparagus cooked in beer is also delicious with Hollandaise sauce.

Serves 4

Carrots in Beer

4 *large carrots*
½ *pint brown ale*
1 *ounce butter*

seasoning to taste
1 *teaspoon castor sugar*

Scrape and slice carrots into long, thin slices. Melt butter in a frying pan, add beer and carrots and cook slowly until tender, shaking frequently. Season to taste and add castor sugar. Cook for another couple of minutes and serve hot.

Serves 4

Brussels Sprouts in Beer

1 *pound fresh Brussels sprouts*
light ale to cover

2 *ounces butter*
seasoning to taste

Trim and wash sprouts. Place in a saucepan and pour over enough beer to cover. Bring to the boil and cook on a medium flame for 20 minutes or until tender. Add more beer from time to time if liquid is disappearing. Drain, season and serve hot with butter on top.

Serves 2–4

Sweet Potato Soufflé

1½ *pounds sweet potatoes (cooked and mashed)*
¼ *pint brown ale*
3 *tablespoons double cream*
4 *tablespoons butter (melted)*
4 *eggs (separated—see p. 137—whites stiffly beaten)*

½ *teaspoon salt*
pinch nutmeg
½ *teaspoon orange rind (grated)*

Heat oven to 400°F, mark 6. Beat the sweet potato, brown ale, cream, butter, egg yolks, salt, nutmeg and orange rind until fluffy. Fold in the egg whites. Turn into a buttered soufflé dish and bake for 25 minutes or until browned and set, and serve at once.

Serves 6

Hawaiian Sweet Potato

2 pounds small sweet
  potatoes
6 slices fresh pineapple

½ pint sweet stout
2 ounces butter
2 tablespoons brown sugar

First boil the sweet potatoes in their skins for about 30 minutes, or until tender. Peel and slice thickly. Peel pineapple slices and lay on the bottom of a shallow baking dish. Lay potato pieces on top, cut side facing down. Melt butter in a small saucepan; add sugar and beer and stir until sugar is dissolved. Pour over potatoes and pineapple and bake at 375°F, mark 4–5, for 30 minutes, basting often. These are delicious served with any roast meat but particularly pork or ham.

Serves 4

Candied Sweet Potatoes

2 pounds sweet potatoes
4 ounces brown sugar
¼ pint brown ale
2 teaspoons orange rind
  (grated)

½ teaspoon salt
½ teaspoon ginger (ground)

Cook sweet potato in boiling water until tender but still firm, then cool, peel and cut in slices not less than half an inch thick. Arrange in a shallow baking dish. Mix remaining ingredients and cook over low heat until sugar melts and is syrupy, stirring frequently. Pour over potatoes and bake in oven at 400°F, mark 6, for 20 minutes, or until browned, turning once.

Serves 6–8

Stuffed Peppers

4 green peppers
4 tomatoes (peeled and
  chopped)
1 medium sized onion
  (grated)

7 ounces rice (cooked)
3 tablespoons butter (melted)
1 teaspoon salt
pinch pepper
¼ pint light ale

Cut a ½-inch piece from the stem end of the peppers and cut out seeds and fibres. Pour boiling water over them and allow to soak for 10 minutes, then drain. Mix together the tomatoes, onion, rice, butter, salt and pepper and stuff the peppers. Stand upright in a buttered baking dish and pour light ale round them. Bake for 40 minutes at 350°F, mark 5, basting frequently.

Serves 4

Cauliflower au Gratin

1 large cauliflower
*½ pound Cheddar cheese
(grated)*
¼ pint light ale

½ clove garlic (crushed)
*2 teaspoons Worcestershire
sauce*

Choose a firm unmarked cauliflower. Remove leaves. Place whole flower in a deep saucepan and cover with water. Bring to the boil and simmer for 15 minutes. Drain and transfer to a well-buttered casserole dish. In a small saucepan, heat the cheese and gradually stir in the beer. Add garlic and Worcestershire sauce and stir until smooth. Pour cheese sauce evenly over cauliflower and cover casserole. Bake at 350°F, mark 4, for 40 minutes or until cauliflower is tender. Serve hot, spooning cheese sauce over each portion.

Serves 4

Courgettes in Beer

4 medium courgettes
¼ pint light ale
1 tablespoon oil
1 clove garlic
*1 green pepper (seeded and
chopped)*

¼ teaspoon salt
¼ teaspoon pepper
½ teaspoon basil
*1 tablespoon chopped
pimento*

Heat oil in a saucepan and brown garlic lightly. Wipe and slice courgettes, add to pan and brown lightly. Add remaining ingredients, cover, and simmer for about 20 minutes, or until courgettes are tender.

Serves 2–3

Cassoulet

*1 pound haricot beans
  (soaked and pre-cooked)*
*½ pound belly of pork (cut
  into cubes)*
2 cloves garlic (crushed)
2 tablespoons butter
*1 pound cooked lamb
  (cubed)*
*¼ pound garlic sausage
  (sliced)*

6 cocktail Frankfurters
1 small tin butter beans
¼ pint brown ale
1 medium tin tomatoes
1 teaspoon sugar
1 dessertspoon tomato purée
bouquet garni
seasoning to taste

Place haricot beans in a large flameproof casserole. Sauté belly of pork in butter with the garlic. Add to casserole with pieces of lamb, garlic sausage and Frankfurters. Pour over beer and enough water to cover. Add bouquet garni and season. Simmer for 15 minutes, adding butter beans for last 5 minutes. Meanwhile, cook tomatoes to a pulp in a saucepan, add tomato purée and sugar. Pour over Cassoulet just before serving and mix in gently. Serve with French bread and butter.

Serves 4

Beer and Treacle Beans

*1 pound haricot beans
  (dried)*
½ pound salt pork (sliced)
4 tablespoons treacle

1½ pints brown ale
1 teaspoon dry mustard
1½ teaspoons onion powder
1½ teaspoons salt

Wash beans, then cover with cold water and soak overnight. Drain. Cover with fresh water, bring to the boil, then cover and cook over low heat for one hour. Drain, putting liquor to one side. Put half the pork on the bottom of a casserole or earthenware pot and add the beans. Mix the brown ale, treacle, mustard, onion powder and salt and pour over the beans, placing remainder of the salt pork on top. Cover and bake in oven at 275°F, mark 1, for six hours, adding enough bean water every hour or so to replace what has baked away. For the last half hour bake without lid.

Serves 6

Beer Ratatouille

2 large onions   *1 tablespoon olive oil*
4 large green peppers   *¼ pint brown ale*
4 large tomatoes   *seasoning to taste*
1 clove garlic (crushed)

Peel and quarter onions. Wipe and slice green peppers and tomatoes. Peel and slice potatoes. Heat oil in a large frying pan and sauté all together with the garlic for a few minutes. Add beer and seasonings. Bring to the boil and simmer for about 35–40 minutes or until vegetables are tender.

Serves 4

Salad Susannah

2 cups lentils (dried)   *12 spring onions (finely*
1 pint light ale   *chopped)*
1 quart water   *1 medium dill pickle*
1 large onion (pierced with   *(chopped)*
   8 cloves)   *½ teaspoon paprika*
2 bay leaves   *2 cups cabbage (raw,*
3 tablespoons oil   *shredded)*
1½ teaspoons salt   *5 medium potatoes (boiled*
2 tablespoons vinegar   *and thinly sliced)*
¼ teaspoon pepper   *1 tablespoon parsley (finely*
½ teaspoon dry mustard   *chopped)*

Place lentils in a large saucepan with water, beer, bay leaves, onion and 1 teaspoon salt. Bring to boil, cover and simmer for ¾ hour. Take out onion and bay leaves. Drain. Make a dressing by mixing vinegar, seasoning, mustard, paprika, spring onions and dill pickle. Arrange cabbage and potato slices on a serving dish and pile lentils in mounds on top. Pour dressing over entire salad. Garnish with parsley and serve chilled.

Serves 6

German Coleslaw

1 firm white cabbage
¼ pint brown ale
1 cup mayonnaise
1 teaspoon salt

¼ teaspoon English mustard (dry)
2 teaspoon onion (finely chopped)

Finely shred cabbage and set aside. Make a salad dressing by combining mayonnaise, beer, salt and mustard. Add onion. Pour mixture over cabbage, mix well and chill for at least ½ hour before serving.

Serves 4

Potato Salad with Beer Dressing

2 pounds potatoes
4 rashers back bacon
1 stick of celery (trimmed and chopped)
1 tablespoon onion (chopped)
2 teaspoons salt
2 ounces butter
2 tablespoons flour

½ teaspoon English mustard (dry)
1 tablespoon castor sugar
½ pint light ale
½ teaspoon Tabasco sauce
2 tablespoons parsley (chopped)

Peel potatoes and boil until barely tender. Grill bacon. Crumble, mix with chopped celery, onion and 1 teaspoon salt; set aside. Blend butter and flour in a large saucepan. Add mustard, sugar and remaining salt. Stir until smooth. Gradually add beer and Tabasco sauce. Bring to the boil stirring continuously. Pour over potatoes and sprinkle with parsley. Mix lightly and let stand 1 hour. Add bacon mixture, and blend gently.

Serves 4

Celery, Olive and Raisin Salad

1 head celery (cut in short pieces)	½ cup onion (chopped)
	¼ pint brown ale
2 ounces black olives (halved and stoned)	1 small carton sour cream
	2 tablespoons chilli sauce
½ cup raisins (chopped)	juice ½ lemon

Mix olives, celery and raisins together in a salad bowl. In a separate bowl mix beer, sour cream, chilli sauce, onion and lemon juice. Pour over salad and chill before serving.

Serves 4

French Bean Salad

¾ pound French beans	⅛ pint brown ale
¾ pound tomatoes	1 teaspoon chives (chopped)
1 cucumber	1 teaspoon parsley (chopped)
1 cup French dressing	black pepper (fresh ground)

Trim beans and remove any strings. Cook in boiling salted water for about 20 minutes or until tender. Refresh and drain. Scald, skin and quarter tomatoes and peel and cube cucumber. Arrange on a serving dish. Mix French dressing, beer, chives, green pepper and parsley together and pour over. Sprinkle liberally with black pepper and chill before serving as a side salad.

Serves 4

Party Beer Tomatoes

1 pound tomatoes	2 tablespoons parsley
1 cup light ale	(finely chopped)

Wash and thinly slice tomatoes. Arrange on a serving dish and pour over beer. Sprinkle with parsley. Serve as a side salad.

Serves 4

Mushroom Salad in Beer

1 pound raw small white
  mushrooms (without
  stalks)
⅔ cup salad oil
⅓ cup brown ale
1 tablespoon lemon juice
1 tablespoon onion (finely
  chopped)

1 tablespoon parsley
  (chopped)
¼ teaspoon Oregano
  (crushed)
½ teaspoon salt
black pepper to taste

Skin and slice mushrooms and lay in a shallow dish. Combine remaining ingredients and pour over mushrooms. Cover tightly and leave to marinate for about 3 hours. Serve as a side salad. These mushrooms will keep for about 1 week if stored in a refrigerator in a sealed jar.

Serves 4

Coleslaw Dressing

3 tablespoons cornflour
½ pint milk
1 teaspoon salt

1 teaspoon mustard
1 tablespoon butter
¼ pint light ale

Mix cornflour and milk in the top of a double boiler and place over hot water, stirring steadily until mixture thickens. Stir in salt, mustard, butter and light ale and cook for 10 minutes, stirring frequently. Serve as dressing for potato salad or coleslaw.

Lager Dressing

4 ounces olive oil
3 tablespoons wine vinegar
3 tablespoons lager
¾ teaspoon salt

⅛ teaspoon black pepper
  (fresh ground)
dash garlic powder

Beat or shake all ingredients together. Delicious with potato, coleslaw or green salads.

Beer Dressing for Potato Salad

1 large onion (diced)	*pinch pepper*
3 tablespoons salad oil	*2 teaspoons sugar*
2 tablespoons flour	*¾ pint light ale*
1½ teaspoons salt	*3 tablespoons cider vinegar*

Sauté the onions in oil for 10 minutes, stirring frequently; blend in flour, salt, pepper and sugar. Gradually add beer and vinegar, stirring constantly to boiling point. Cook over low heat for five minutes. Cool slightly and pour over potatoes.

Serves 6

Cheese and Cheese Dishes

BEER AND cheese have always gone together. Everyone knows that the taste of cheese, sharp or mild, is happily enriched by the addition of beer. Some superb new varieties of cheese have been created over the years by the inclusion of beer. You can have great fun (as well as rewarding results) in making the beer cheeses included in this chapter and in experimenting with beer and your own favourite cheese. Who knows, you might come up with a cheese as successful as Ilchester!

Everybody has their own favourite recipe for Welsh Rarebit with beer and here you will find a selection of the best. Again this is an area where you can successfully experiment in inventing your own beer recipes. Remember when making rarebits or fondues, or any dish with melted cheese, that the condition of the cheese is important. If you use stale cheese you will get a tough, elastic consistency which will ruin the recipe. Cheese dishes are *not* intended as a way of using up scraps.

In the following pages you will find in addition to cheeses, rarebits and fondues, an exciting selection of cheese snacks, savouries, dips, spreads and flans.

Mexican Rarebit

$1\frac{1}{2}$ cups brown ale
1 cup Gruyère cheese (grated)
1 ounce butter

1 tablespoon flour
$\frac{1}{2}$ teaspoon chilli powder
pinch cayenne pepper
$\frac{1}{2}$ teaspoon salt

Melt butter in a saucepan, add flour and blend together thoroughly. Gradually add beer and gradually stir over low flame until
beginning to thicken. Add cheese and continue to stir until
melted. Add chilli powder and cayenne pepper. Serve hot on
buttered toast.

Serves 4

Shrimp Rarebit

¾ *pound Cheddar cheese*   ¾ *cup shrimps (cooked)*
  (grated)   *1 tablespoon onion (finely*
1 cup light ale   *chopped)*
1 ounce butter   *1 tablespoon chives*
½ *teaspoon paprika*   *(snipped)*
1 teaspoon English mustard
  (dry)

Melt cheese and butter in a saucepan. Add paprika, mustard and
beer, stirring constantly. When mixture is smooth, add shrimps
and onion. Continue stirring until heated through. Serve on toast,
garnished with chives.

Serves 4–5

Worcester Rarebit

½ *pound Cheddar cheese*   *1 teaspoon paprika*
  (grated)   *dash Worcestershire sauce*
¼ *pint brown ale*
½ *teaspoon English*
  mustard (dry)

Mix mustard, paprika and Worcestershire sauce in a saucepan.
Add beer and heat through on a low heat. Stir in the cheese until
it has melted taking care not to over-heat. Serve on toast.

Serves 4

Mustard Rarebit

1 pound Cheddar cheese
¼ pint brown ale
1 teaspoon French mustard
1 teaspoon German mustard
1 teaspoon English mustard (made)

1 tablespoon cornflour
1 tablespoon cold water
1 ounce butter
4–5 slices toast

Mix French, German and English mustards together. Grate cheese. Melt butter in a saucepan and add cheese and beer. Stir continuously until cheese is melted. Mix cornflour to a paste with cold water and stir into cheese to thicken. Blend in mustard, pour over toast and pop under the grill to brown before serving.

Serves 4–5

Lancashire Rarebit

¾ pound Lancashire cheese
3 tablespoons brown ale
2 eggs (hard boiled)

1 ounce butter
4 slices toast
paprika to garnish

Grate the cheese. Slice the hard-boiled eggs. Melt butter in a saucepan and add cheese and beer. Cook, stirring continuously, until cheese has melted. Arrange slices of egg on toast and pour hot cheese mixture over. Pop under grill to brown. Sprinkle with paprika and serve hot. A successful variation of this recipe for anchovy addicts is to replace the eggs with anchovy paste spread on the toast before covering with cheese mixture.

Serves 4

Banana Welsh Rarebit

4 bananas
½ pound Cheddar cheese
1 ounce butter
3 tablespoons lager
pinch salt
½ teaspoon English mustard
  (dry)

1 egg (beaten)
pinch cayenne pepper
parsley to garnish
4 slices toast

Cut each banana into quarters. Salt lightly and gently fry in half the butter until soft. Meanwhile, cut toast into triangles and arrange in a large serving dish. Cover with bananas and keep hot. Grate cheese. Melt remaining butter in a saucepan and add cheese, lager and cayenne pepper, stirring until smooth. Add beaten egg and cook until mixture thickens. Pour over banana toasts; garnish with parsley and serve at once.

Serves 4

Cheese Muff

½ pound Cheshire cheese
2 tablespoons brown ale
1 egg

1 ounce butter
black pepper (fresh ground)
toast slices to serve

Grate cheese. Beat egg in a bowl and set aside. Melt butter in a saucepan and add cheese and beer. Cook until cheese is melted, stirring continuously. Add egg and continue to cook still stirring until egg scrambles in the cheese. Serve on hot toast liberally sprinkled with black pepper.

Serves 4

English Monkey

½ pound Cheddar cheese
2 tablespoons lager
1 cup stale breadcrumbs
  (see p. 137)

½ pint milk
1 egg
½ ounce butter
seasoning to taste

Cut cheese into small pieces. Soak breadcrumbs in milk for $\frac{1}{4}$ hour. Strain off excess milk. Beat egg and set aside. Melt butter in a pan and add cheese and lager. When cheese is melted mix in breadcrumbs and egg and season. Cook for 3–4 minutes until scrambled. Serve with triangles of hot toast for a substantial snack.

Serves 4

Beer Fondue (1)

1 pound Gouda cheese (grated)	*$\frac{1}{2}$ clove garlic (crushed)*
$\frac{1}{2}$ pint light ale	*salt and cayenne pepper to taste*
1 tablespoon cornflour	*French bread to serve*

Well butter a fireproof casserole or pan and heat the beer and cheese over a low heat until all the cheese has melted. Add crushed garlic and seasoning. Blend the cornflour with a little beer and add to the mixture. Allow to thicken stirring continuously. Keep hot over a low heat (preferably in a fondue pan). Each guest serves himself with a fork, dipping pieces of French bread into the beer fondue.

Serves 4

Beer Fondue (2)

$\frac{1}{2}$ pound Cheddar cheese (grated)	*$1\frac{1}{2}$ cups lager*
$\frac{1}{2}$ pound Gruyère cheese (grated)	*dash Tabasco sauce*
1 clove garlic	*black pepper to taste*
	French bread (to serve)

Mix grated cheeses together and season with black pepper. Rub garlic clove all round the fondue pot and pour in beer. Heat gently on top of stove, gradually adding cheese mixture. Stir continuously until melted. Add Tabasco sauce. Serve in a fondue pot over flame to keep hot, with chunks of French bread for dipping. Add a little more beer from time to time at the table if mixture is getting too thick.

Serves 4

Gloucester Cheese in Ale

½ pound Double Gloucester   ½ pint light ale
   cheese   4 slices thick white bread
English mustard (made)

Heat oven to 350°F, mark 4. Slice cheese and spread slices with
mustard. Lay side by side, mustard side up, in a casserole dish.
Pour beer over and bake until cheese melts. Meanwhile, toast
bread and when cheese is ready pour over the bread. Basically a
rarebit variation this makes a delicious quick snack.

Serves 4

Home-made Camembert

1 pound Cheddar cheese   4 tablespoons cold water
3 tablespoons brown ale

Line a terrine with butter muslin and press cheese into it. Cover
with more butter muslin and sprinkle with 1 tablespoon cold
water. Cover with a lid which has a hole in it to allow cheese to
breathe (if you cannot get a terrine with a hole in the lid use foil
and pierce a few holes in it). Leave to mature for 4 days, sprinkling with water once a day. On the fifth, sixth and seventh days
sprinkle with brown ale. At the end of this time you will have a
superb home-made Camembert-style cheese with a light crust
on top.

Chive and Parsley Cheese

1 pound Cheddar cheese   6 chives
½ pint light ale   2 sprigs parsley

Place cheese in an earthenware or china pot a little longer than itself and pour over as much beer as possible without it overflowing.
Leave cheese overnight to absorb beer. Remove from pot and
work to a soft consistency with a little more beer. Snip chives into

Iced Cucumber Soup (page 8)

small pieces, chop parsley (without stalks) and mix into cheese mixture. Pile into pot and moisten again with beer. Leave for another 24 hours and moisten again with beer. Leave for 4 days, sprinkling occasionally with beer, until a skin forms on top when it is ready to eat.

Potted Cheese

¾ pound red Cheshire   ¼ teaspoon curry powder
   cheese   pinch mace (powdered)
2 ounces butter   clarified butter (see p. 139)
2 tablespoons brown ale

Cream the cheese and butter with a wooden spoon. Gradually add the beer, curry powder and mace. Pack tightly into a pot and pour over a little clarified butter to seal from the air.

Bier Kase

¼ pound Roquefort cheese   1 tablespoon onion (grated)
¾ pound Cheddar cheese   ½ pint brown ale
1 ounce butter   Worcestershire sauce to taste
½ teaspoon English mustard   pinch salt
   (dry)

Grate Cheddar and cream with butter and Roquefort in a bowl. Add onion, Worcestershire sauce, mustard and salt. Mix thoroughly, gradually adding the beer. Serve chilled on thin sliced black or rye bread.

   Serves 4

Crème Bonbel

1 Bonbel cheese   ¼ pound butter
¼ pint brown ale   1 tablespoon onion (grated)
½ teaspoon English mustard   2 sprigs parsley (finely
   (dry)   chopped)

Beer Fondue (page 85)

With a very sharp knife carefully cut round the top skin of the cheese, so that it can be removed like a lid. Set aside. Carefully cut cheese inside into portions which can be easily levered out without breaking the skin shell. Cream the cheese in an electric blender with the butter. Beat in the beer, mustard, onion and chopped parsley. Stuff the Bonbel shell with the cheese mixture and use 'lid' to cut out a few leaves or flower shapes to decorate the top. Chill before using with crackers, toast or as a sandwich filling.

Austrian Cheese Spread

1 pound cream cheese	*1 tablespoon chives (chopped)*
3 tablespoons light ale	*1 tablespoon capers*
¼ pound butter	*(chopped)*
2 tablespoons sour cream	*1 teaspoon caraway seeds*
1 teaspoon paprika	

Beat the cream cheese, beer, butter and sour cream together. Add paprika, chives, capers and caraway seeds. Chill before using. Good on crackers, for party snacks of all kinds and as a sandwich filling.

Cheese Dip (1)

1 pound cream cheese	*1 clove garlic (chopped)*
¼ cup lager	*1 small can pimento*
2 medium onions (chopped)	*(chopped)*
2 tablespoons salad oil	*2 small cans green peppers*
2 medium tomatoes	*(chopped)*
(chopped)	*2 tablespoons condensed milk*

Sauté onions in oil but do not brown. Add tomatoes, garlic, pimentos and peppers and simmer for ¾ hour. Stir in condensed milk and cheese and when cheese is melted add beer. Serve in a bowl with crisps to dip into the mixture. Delicious for cocktail parties.

Cheese Dip (2)

2 tablespoons brown ale
½ pound cream cheese
1 tablespoon green olives
  (finely chopped)

1 teaspoon celery salt

Mix cream cheese with a little of the beer and stir well. Add olives and celery salt. Stir again and add more beer until dipping consistency. Serve with celery sticks and raw carrots as a party dip.

Cheese Dip (3)

2 pounds Cheddar cheese
  (grated)
4 ounces Roquefort cheese
1 teaspoon English mustard
  (dry)

1 teaspoon Worcestershire
  sauce
1 tablespoon onion
  (chopped)
½ pint brown ale

Cream Roquefort cheese with a little of the beer in a bowl. Add remaining ingredients and blend together slowly with an electric blender. Cover and chill for a couple of hours at least before serving with crackers.

Cheese Dip (4)

½ pound cottage cheese
¼ pound blue cheese
  (crumbled)
3 tablespoons brown ale
1 teaspoon Worcestershire
  sauce

½ clove garlic, crushed
1 tablespoon black olives
  (chopped)
1 tablespoon almonds
  (chopped)

Cream blue cheese and cream cheese together with a little beer. Add remaining ingredients. If dip is not thin enough increase the amount of beer as desired. Serve with flowers of raw cauliflower to dip into bowl.

Cheese and Bacon Creams

4 rashers streaky bacon
2 eggs
¼ pint brown ale
¼ pint double cream
¾ cup Gruyère cheese
  (grated)

¼ cup Parmesan cheese
  (grated)
seasoning to taste

Fry rashers of bacon and chop into small pieces. Beat the eggs cream and beer together and add cheeses, seasoning and bacon. Pour into individual ramekins. Heat oven to 425°F, mark 6 and cook in a bain-marie for about 20 minutes. To test if creams are done: insert a knife into the centre which should come out clean if they are ready.

Serves 6

Sallé

1¼ cups Gruyère cheese
  (grated)
2 tablespoons butter
1 tablespoon onion (finely
  chopped)
2½ tablespoons plain flour

⅜ pint light ale
3 eggs (beaten)
½ teaspoon salt
¼ pint double cream
8 ounces shortcrust pastry
  (see p. 138)

Have ready the shortcrust pastry and line into a flan case. Sauté onion in the butter in a saucepan until just soft. Blend in flour and salt. Gradually add beer and cream and bring to the boil stirring constantly. When beer sauce has cooled a little add cheese and eggs; season and turn into flan case. Heat oven to 400°F, mark 6, and bake for about ½ hour or until browned and set.

Serves 3–4

Beer and Bacon Croque

4 rashers back bacon   2 tablespoons chutney
¾ pound Cheddar cheese   4 slices toast
3 tablespoons lager
Worcestershire sauce to
   taste

Grate cheese and melt in a saucepan with the beer and Worcester-shire sauce. Grill bacon. Butter toast slices and pour cheese over 2 slices. Put a tablespoon of chutney on each and lay 2 rashers of bacon on top. Sandwich with remaining toast slices and serve hot.

Serves 2

French Beer Toast

6 slices white bread   2 teaspoons flour
¼ pint brown ale   1 teaspoon paprika
3 eggs   2 ounces butter
¼ pound Cheddar cheese
   (grated)

Beat the eggs lightly and add grated cheese, flour and paprika. Mix well. Soak the bread in the beer and spread half the cheese mixture on one side of the beer-soaked slices. Heat butter in a frying pan and place bread, cheese side down in it. Fry until golden. Spread remaining mixture on other side of each slice. Then turn and fry on this side too. Cut into fingers and serve hot as a savoury snack.

Serves 4

Danish Cheese Balls

1 pound Danish blue   1 teaspoon Worcestershire
   cheese   sauce
½ pound cream cheese   dash Tabasco sauce
1 tablespoon chives (finely   2 tablespoons brown ale
   snipped)   1½ cups walnuts (chopped)

Cream Danish Blue and cream cheese together in a bowl. Mix in chives, Worcestershire sauce, Tabasco sauce, and beer. Stir well and chill for about 1 hour in the refrigerator. Shape into small balls and roll in chopped nuts. Keep chilled until serving time. Serve as cocktail snacks.

Gouda Puffs

4 ounces Gouda cheese
   (shredded)
2 tablespoons light ale
2½ tablespoons water
5 ounces butter

1 ounce flour
1 egg
pinch salt
French mustard

Bring water, beer, 1 ounce butter and salt to the boil. Add all the flour at once. Stir until mixture thickens and sticks together. Remove from heat. Add egg, beating it into the mixture. With 2 teaspoons form small balls, the size of marbles; place them on a greased baking sheet 2 inches apart and bake in a hot oven 400°F, mark 5, for 10–15 minutes. Take care not to open oven door for at least 10 minutes or puffs will collapse. Soften remaining butter with cheese and flavour with French mustard. Cut puffs open and fill with this mixture. Serve as cocktail savouries.

Makes 25–30 puffs

Cheese Cones

4 ounces Cheddar cheese
   (grated)
2 ounces breadcrumbs
4 slices French bread
   (about 1 inch thick)
1 tablespoon lager

1 tablespoon milk
½ ounce butter (melted)
1 egg yolk (to separate—
   see p. 137)
black pepper to taste
pinch cayenne pepper

Melt half the butter. Mix the breadcrumbs, milk, beer, egg yolk, cheese, melted butter, pepper and cayenne together. Make a hollow in the centre of each slice of bread. Fry the bread on both sides in remaining butter and drain. Pile the cheese mixture into the slices of bread, forming cones. Pre-heat oven to 325°F, mark 2–3, and pop cones in to brown. These make unusual party appetisers.

Makes 4

Cheese Pancakes

¼ *pound Edam cheese*	*1 egg yolk (to separate—*
3 tablespoons brown ale	*see p. 137)*
4 ounces plain flour	¼ *pint milk*
1 egg	*1 ounce butter*

Sift the flour with salt in a bowl; add the egg and egg yolk and gradually add the milk, stirring all the time. Melt 1 ounce butter and stir in. Add the beer and beat well. Batter should be the consistency of thin cream—if too thick, add a little more beer. Grate the cheese and mix well into the batter. Let the batter stand for ½ hour. Heat remaining butter in a pan and pour in 1 tablespoon of the mixture, rolling it round immediately. Cook until the bottom is golden and then toss over to cook second side. Repeat for subsequent pancakes. Serve hot. These make a delicious savoury or can be filled with ham for a party snack.

Serves 4

Desserts

PERHAPS THIS is the area where you least expected to find beer playing a useful part in your cooking? Nothing could be further from the truth. Whether your taste inclines to rich puddings, pies or pancakes or the lighter flans and fruit sweets, your desserts (like your cakes) will benefit from the enriching, lightening and preserving qualities of beer. (For example, christmas puddings, with beer included, last longer.)

Nearly all the sweets in this section can be made in advance and served either cold or re-heated easily before serving. Even the pancakes can be made the day before and successfully warmed up when you are ready to eat them. To re-heat pancakes simply bake them in the oven for 4–5 minutes at 300°F, mark 4, laid overlapping on a buttered baking sheet with more melted butter brushed over them. They will come out looking freshly made.

Fresh fruit too is delicious marinated in beer. Try experimenting with a little light ale or lager poured over your own fruit salad mixture. Peaches and pears respond particularly well to this treatment and apples baked in beer are delicious.

Rich Christmas Pudding

½ pound self-raising flour
¾ pound breadcrumbs (fresh
  white—see p. 137)
1 pound currants
1 pound sultanas
1 pound raisins (stoned)
¾ pound suet (shredded)
¼ pound candied peel
  (chopped)
2 ounces almonds (shredded)

1 apple (peeled and grated)
juice 1 orange
rind 1 orange (grated)
1 teaspoon mixed spice
½ nutmeg (grated)
1 teaspoon salt
6 eggs (well beaten)
¼ pint stout
½ pound brown sugar

Have ready well greased pudding basins and saucepans of boiling water large enough to immerse the puddings. Sift the flour with the salt and spices in a very large basin. Add breadcrumbs, fruit, peel, almonds, suet and brown sugar and mix well together. Beat eggs, stout and orange juice together and stir well into pudding mixture. Turn into basins.

Cover puddings with buttered greaseproof paper and then foil (with a pleat to allow for swelling). Tie down securely leaving loops either side to facilitate removing puddings from saucepan. Boil puddings for 6 hours if you make large ones or 4 hours for small ones. Take care not to let them go off the boil and add boiling water from time to time as necessary. Leave to go cold; remove covering and replace with fresh greaseproof and foil before storing. Boil for a further 2 hours when ready to use. Serve with brandy or rum butter.

Makes 4 small or 2 large puddings

Spicy Christmas Pudding

1 pound flour
1 pound breadcrumbs
  (fresh white—see p. 137)
1¼ pounds sultanas
1¼ pounds currants
1 pound raisins
4 ounces almonds
1 nutmeg (grated)

1 pound mixed peel
1 pound beef suet (shredded)
1 teaspoon mixed spice
1 teaspoon ginger (ground)
1 pound brown sugar
8 eggs
½ pint light ale
1 wineglass brandy

Have ready well greased pudding basins and saucepans of boiling water, large enough to immerse puddings. Stone fruit. Chop peel and almonds. Mix flour, spices, suet, fruit, sugar and bread-crumbs in a large bowl. Beat eggs to a froth and add to mixture with beer. Turn into pudding basins and cover and cook as for Rich Christmas Pudding (*see* page 96). When cool pour a little brandy over each pudding before storing.

Makes 4 medium or 2 large puddings

Raisin Pudding

1½ pounds plain flour
1¼ pounds raisins (stoned)
1¼ pounds suet (shredded)
1 egg (beaten)

1¼ pounds brown sugar
old ale to mix
¼ teaspoon bicarbonate soda

Have ready a well greased pudding basin. Mix flour, suet, raisins, sugar and egg together. Add enough ale to mix smoothly. Dissolve the bicarbonate of soda in a little ale and beat into mixture. Pile into pudding basin and cover as for Rich Christmas Pudding (*see* page 96). Steam for 4 hours and serve hot with custard.

Serves 6

Date Delight

4 ounces self raising flour   *½ teaspoon mixed spice*
4 ounces dates (stoned and   *2 tablespoons demerara*
  chopped)   *sugar*
4 tablespoons breadcrumbs   *1 tablespoon milk*
  (fresh white—see p. 137)   *2 eggs*
3 ounces butter   *pinch salt*
1–2 tablespoons light ale

Have ready a well greased pudding basin. Mix flour, spice, salt
and breadcrumbs in a bowl. Rub in butter and add sugar and
dates, stirring well. Mix in one tablespoon beer. Beat eggs and
syrup in a separate bowl and mix into pudding until smooth,
adding a little more beer if necessary. Turn into basin and cover
with buttered greaseproof paper and foil, leaving a pleat in the
centre to allow for swelling. Tie down securely and steam 1½–2
hours. Serve with custard.

Buckinghamshire Florentine

8 ounces quantity shortcrust   *3 tablespoons sugar*
  pastry (see p. 139)   *¼ pint light ale*
1½ pounds apples   *icing sugar to dust*
½ pint water

Have ready the shortcrust pastry. Line a pie dish with it (leaving
enough to make the pastry top) and bake blind (*see* page 139).
Bring sugar and water to the boil together. Peel, core and slice
apples and cook in the sugar syrup until just translucent. Pile into
pie dish. Cover with remaining pastry, sealing the edges and
pricking a few holes in the top. Sprinkle with icing sugar. Cook
in a pre-heated oven at 400°F, mark 5–6, for about 20 minutes or
until top pastry is golden. Meanwhile, heat the beer in a pan.
When pie is cooked cut one small wedge just before serving and
pour in the hot beer.

Serves 4

Apple Dragons

4 large cooking apples   *1 ounce butter*
2 ounces demerara sugar   *¼ pint brown ale*
*2 ounces sultanas (seeded
    and chopped*

Wash and core apples and place in a shallow baking dish. Mix together sugar and sultanas and pile into centres of apples. Pour
over beer and sprinkle a little more sugar in the beer in the bottom
of the baking dish. Cook in the oven at 375°F, mark 5, for about
¾–1 hour. Serve hot with a little of the syrup spooned over.

Serves 4

Peach and Pear Salad

4 fresh peaches   *¼ pint lager*
small bunch black grapes   *¼ pint double cream*
2 ripe pears

Peel and quarter peaches and pears. De-pip and halve grapes.
Arrange fruits in coupe glasses and pour over lager. Whip cream
and place a large spoonful on top of sweet. Chill before serving.

Serves 2

Peach Trifle

6 ripe peaches (fresh)   *½ pint custard (powdered)*
¼ pint lager or light ale   *¼ pint double cream*
6 sponge fingers

Peel, stone and quarter peaches. Arrange sponge fingers on the
bottom of a decorative glass bowl and lay peach quarters on top.
Pour beer over. Make up custard according to instructions on the
packet and pour carefully on to trifle. Leave to cool and, when
set, decorate with whipped cream. Serve chilled.

Serves 4

Vanilla Cream Flan

8 ounces quantity shortcrust
   pastry (see p. 139)
$\frac{1}{3}$ cup plain flour
$\frac{1}{2}$ cup sugar
6 egg yolks
pinch salt

$\frac{3}{4}$ pint lager
$\frac{1}{2}$ pint milk (scalded)
1 teaspoon vanilla essence
$\frac{1}{4}$ pint double cream
grated chocolate to decorate

Roll out shortcrust pastry; line flan tin and bake blind (*see* page
139). Beat egg yolks and mix with flour, sugar and salt in a saucepan. Cook over a low heat gradually stirring in milk and beer.
When thick add vanilla and leave to cool. Whip cream and fold in.
Turn into flan case and decorate with grated chocolate.

Danish Pancakes

$\frac{1}{2}$ pound plain flour
1 level tablespoon castor
   sugar
2 eggs
$\frac{1}{8}$ pint lager

$\frac{1}{8}$ pint single cream
$\frac{1}{4}$ pint milk
cranberry or redcurrant
   jelly
2 ounces butter

Stir beaten egg yolks, beer and cream into the flour, add sugar
and milk and beat to a smooth batter. Stiffly whip and fold in the
egg whites. Pour all the batter into a very large hot lightly
greased pan. Cook until firm beneath, finish under a medium hot
grill. Carefully turn the whole large cake on to a sugared paper,
spread very quickly with softened butter and jelly. Roll up like a
Swiss roll; serve cut into slices about an inch in thickness with
more jelly as required.

Makes 6–8 pancakes

Viennese Pancakes

1 pound self-raising flour
2 eggs
3 tablespoons butter
$\frac{1}{2}$ pint milk

$\frac{1}{4}$ pint brown ale
2 tablespoons brown sugar
$\frac{1}{4}$ teaspoon grated nutmeg

Melt two-thirds of the butter in a bowl and set aside. Sift flour with nutmeg, add sugar; stir in beaten eggs, milk, butter and beer and beat all very thoroughly. Drop large spoonfuls on to a very hot pan or girdle plate, lightly greased with butter. Turn when firm and cook on other side. Serve with cream and red-currant jelly.

Makes 8–10 pancakes

French Pancakes

2 ounces flour
2 ounces sugar
2 eggs
2 ounces butter

¼ pint milk
¼ pint brown ale
jam of your choice for
    filling

Heat milk and beer; cream butter; beat eggs and mix the flour with the beaten eggs, adding the creaming and pouring on the beer and milk. Allow to stand for one hour. Pour into small flan tins and bake at 450°F, mark 7, for ¼ hour. Meanwhile, heat the jam. Turn the pancakes out, spread with jam and serve at once.

Makes 6–8 pancakes

Beer Waffles

3 cups plain flour
½ cup oil
2 eggs
¾ pint light ale
1 tablespoon lemon rind
    (grated)

1 teaspoon vanilla essence
1 teaspoon lemon juice
½ pint double cream
pinch salt
1½ tablespoons soft brown
    sugar

Mix flour, beer and oil in a large bowl. Add eggs, lemon juice and rind, vanilla essence, cream, salt and sugar. Beat well and leave to stand for at least 2 hours. Spread batter thinly on a hot, buttered waffle iron and cook until crisp. Serve with orange sauce (*see* page 134) or New England Pilgrims' Syrup (*see* page 134).

Serves 6

Flapjacks

6 ounces flour (sifted)
¾ teaspoon salt
1½ teaspoons strong baking
   powder
2 teaspoons sugar
1 egg white (stiffly beaten)

2 egg yolks
2 tablespoons butter
   (melted)
¼ pint lager
¼ pint milk

Sift together flour, salt, baking powder and sugar. Beat together
egg yolks, butter, beer and milk. Add to flour mixture, stirring
until smooth. Fold in egg white. Drop tablespoonful at a time on
to hot girdle or heavy pan, well-greased. Bake until bubbles
cover the top, then turn and bake until browned on the other side.
Serve with hot Pilgrims' Syrup (*see* page 134) or maple syrup.

Makes about 18 pancakes

Peach Fritters

6 peaches
1 cup flour
2 eggs separated—see
   p. 137)
1½ tablespoons butter

¼ pint light ale
pinch salt
½ teaspoon sugar
oil for deep frying
whipped cream to serve

Stone and halve peaches. Make a batter by mixing together egg
yolks, beer, butter, salt and sugar. Beat until smooth. Beat egg
whites separately until they stand up in peaks and fold into batter
mixture. Heat oil in a deep fryer to 350°F. Dip peach halves in
batter and drop into hot oil. Fry until golden. Serve hot with
whipped cream.

Makes 12 fritters

Beer and Banana Fritters

2 bananas
4 ounces flour
1 egg
pinch salt

¼ pint brown ale
¼ pint milk
castor sugar for sprinkling
pinch cinnamon

Beat the bananas to a pulp and mix the remaining ingredients into a batter. Cook the batter as for pancakes but when one side is cooked, spread on the banana pulp and sprinkle with castor sugar and cinnamon. As the other side cooks, roll up each pancake. Serve hot.

Makes 4 fritters

Cheesecake with Beer

8 eggs	*6 ounces flour*
10 ounces butter	*15–17 fluid ounces light ale*
4 pounds dry cheese	*3 lemon rinds*
¾ pound sugar	
½ pound currants or	
sultanas or mixed fruit	

First line a flan case with shortcrust pastry (*see* page 139). Grate the lemon rinds finely and grate the cheese to a fine powder in a bowl. Mix in the flour, sugar and eggs and melt the fat, adding this with the beer. Stir in the grated lemon peel and fruits. Turn this filling into the flan case and bake in a moderate oven, 375°F, mark 5, for ¾ hour.

Baking Breads and Cakes

FOR MOST aspiring cooks baking, particularly bread-making, is the true heart of home cooking. In an age when everything can be bought ready made, frozen or dried, there is something particularly attractive about the idea of making our own bread.

There is nothing like the smell and taste of fresh home-made bread and made with beer it is truly mouth watering. Beer helps the dough rise, improves the texture of the crust and imparts a delicious flavour to the finished bread.

Breadmaking is not as difficult as it sounds and if you follow the stages carefully you should have no trouble in baking success-ful loaves. There are four stages: (1) Sponging. The yeast is dis-solved in all the liquid; the flour and salt sifted in a warm bowl; a well is made in the centre and the yeast and liquid poured in. Enough flour is then drawn into the liquid from the sides to make a thick batter. It is covered with a damp cloth and left in a warm place for about 20 minutes to rise. (2) Rising. The remaining flour is drawn into the dough and kneaded well before being transferred to a thoroughly greased bowl and turned a couple of times to ensure that all the surface is evenly covered. Cover again with a damp cloth and leave it to rise in a warm place until the dough is twice its original size. It is now ready to shape as you wish. (3) Proving. Another period of rising but this time it is left for about 20 minutes in a hotter place (such as over the stove or in the oven warming drawer) until it starts to swell. (4) The last stage of course is baking.

Cakes made with beer are rich, subtly flavoured and light in texture. In cake-making, proper preparation of ingredients and utensils is very important. All dried fruit should be carefully cleaned because gritty fruit will spoil both the flavour and texture of your cake. Nuts should be prepared according to the recipe. If it says shredded almonds it means shredded (not chopped or split). It is surprising what a difference this kind of variation can make to the appearance and texture of the cake.

A properly prepared cake tin should have the sides and bottom brushed with melted fat and then it should be lined with well buttered greaseproof paper—*cut to shape*, not just squashed in. Cut a circle of greaseproof to line the base and a strip about an inch larger and an inch wider than the circumference of the tin to line the sides. Fold ½ inch over at the bottom of the strip and make ½-inch cuts in this fold so that, when the paper is lined into the tin, it will overlap and lie flat on the bottom, under the circular base of greaseproof.

Equally important is the way you arrange your cakes in the oven. A centre shelf is the best position for baking a cake, and if you are making more than one cake arrange them side by side leaving room for the heat to circulate around the cakes or baking sheets, otherwise your cakes will have burnt bases.

A word of warning: when using beer in mixing a cake take great care that the mixture does not become too wet—you may find that the quantities given can be slightly reduced. It is better to use too little beer than too much.

Beer Bread

½–¾ *ounce fresh yeast*	*1 dessertspoon salt*
½ *teaspoon sugar*	½ *pint water*
2 *pounds plain flour*	½ *pint brown ale*

Cream the yeast with the sugar and add to the water and beer. Sift flour and salt into warm mixing bowl; make a well in the centre. Warm liquid and yeast and pour in, drawing enough flour into the liquid to form a thick batter. Sprinkle top with flour, cover with a damp cloth and leave to rise for about ¼ hour in a warm place. Work remaining flour in by hand to form dough and knead well on a floured surface. Lightly grease a large warm bowl (make sure it is large enough to leave the dough plenty of rising room) and place dough in it, turning a couple of times to grease whole surface. Make a light cross cut in top, cover with a damp cloth and leave for about 1½ hours in a warm place until double its size. Knead dough lightly again on a floured surface and cut in half. Heat oven to 425°F, mark 7. Shape loaves. Grease 2 loaf tins and put dough into them, cover with a cloth and leave to prove for another ¼ hour. Bake for 25 minutes, then lower heat to 400°F, mark 6, for a further 10–15 minutes baking, when loaves should be slightly shrunk from the sides of the tins and well-browned. Tip out onto a rack to cool.

Makes 2 loaves

Swedish Limpa Bread

¾ *pint light ale*	*1 pound white flour (sifted)*
2 tablespoons brown sugar	*½ pound rye flour (sifted)*
2 tablespoons salad oil	*1 tablespoon salt*
3 tablespoons treacle	*2 teaspoons orange rind*
¼ teaspoon aniseed (seed)	*(grated)*
½ ounce yeast	*1 teaspoon cornflour*
6 ounces water (lukewarm)	

Bring to boil two-thirds of the light ale with brown sugar, oil, molasses and aniseed. Cook over low heat for five minutes then cool. Soften yeast in water in a large bowl. Stir in beer mixture and white flour and beat until smooth. Cover with a towel and let rise in a warm place until double in bulk, about 30 minutes. Work in rye flour, salt and orange rind until smooth. Cover and let rise in a warm place until bulk is doubled, about 45 minutes. Turn dough out on to lightly floured surface and knead until very smooth. Divide dough into two. Loaves may be round or long, or one of each. For round loaves tuck edges under to form a smooth top and put in well-greased 8-inch pie plates. Cut ¼-inch gashes at regular intervals (about 2–3 inches) around the loaves. For long loaves roll into rectangle about 12 × 15 inches. Roll up like a swiss roll, sealing edges well after each turn. Place on well-greased baking sheets and cut ¼-inch diagonal gashes 2 inches apart. Mix cornflour with remaining beer and cook over low heat until slightly thickened. Cool. Brush tops of loaves with this glaze, cover and let rise until doubled in bulk, about 45 minutes. Brush again with glaze and bake in oven 350°F, mark 4, for 50 minutes or until browned. Cool on a cake rack, out of draught for smooth top, in draught for cracked top.

Sour Rye Bread

½ ounce yeast
1 tablespoon sugar
2 ounces lukewarm water
½ pound white flour (sifted)
1¼ pounds rye flour
2 ounces whole wheat flour
8 fluid ounces sour milk or buttermilk
3 fluid ounces light ale
2 teaspoons salt
3 tablespoons caraway seeds (optional)

Combine yeast, sugar and water; let soften for 5 minutes. Stir in about one-quarter of the white flour and let stand until bubbles form. Add the remaining white flour, rye flour, whole wheat flour, sour milk, beer, salt and caraway seeds, mixing until a dough is formed. Knead on a lightly-floured surface until smooth and elastic, about 10 minutes. Put the dough into a floured bowl, cover with a towel and let rise in a warm place until doubled in bulk, about 1½ hours. Knead and form into two loaves or one loaf and rolls. Place the loaves in buttered tins or rolls on buttered baking tray, cover and let rise again until doubled in bulk. Bake for 15 minutes in oven at 400°F, mark 6, then reduce heat to 350°, mark 4, and bake for 1¼ hours longer, or until browned. Rolls will require about 35 minutes.

Date-nut Bread

½ pint light ale
¼ pound dates (chopped)
7 ounces flour (sifted)
½ teaspoon salt
1½ teaspoons baking soda
4 tablespoons butter
6 ounces dark brown sugar
2 eggs
4 ounces walnuts (chopped)

Pre-heat oven to 350°F, mark 4. Bring beer and dates to the boil and let cool. Sift together flour, salt and baking soda. Cream butter and brown sugar and beat until light and fluffy; beat in eggs. Alternately add flour mixture and beer and dates mixture, beating after each addition. Stir in the nuts. Bake in 10-inch buttered loaf tin for 55 minutes or until skewer or steel knitting needle comes out clean. Carefully remove from tin and allow to cool on a cake rack. Allow to stand 24 hours before serving.

Hush Puppies

½ pound yellow corn meal
2 teaspoons strong baking
   powder
¾ teaspoon salt
1 medium onion (grated)

1 egg
½ pint milk
2 fluid ounces lager
oil or fat for frying

Mix together corn meal, baking powder, salt and onion in a bowl; lightly beat egg, milk and beer and stir into corn meal mixture. Shape into balls or ovals. Heat oil or fat 2 inches deep in heavy pan and fry Hush Puppies until browned on both sides. Serve hot with fried fish, ham, or bacon.

Serves 6–8

Cheese Brioche (Gannat)

½ ounce yeast
½ cup water (lukewarm)
½ pound flour (sifted)
½ teaspoon salt
3 eggs

3 egg yolks
¼ pound butter (softened)
2 fluid ounces light ale
4 ounces Swiss cheese (diced)

Soften the yeast in water for 5 minutes. Sift about 3 ounces of flour into a small bowl and add yeast until a firm dough is formed. Place the dough in a deep bowl filled with warm water and let rise until floats to the top. Sift remaining salt and flour into a bowl. Beat together eggs and egg yolks and add to the flour with the butter and beer. Work together with the hand until a soft dough is formed, then work in the cheese. Punch down and turn into a buttered 9-inch tin about 2 inches deep.

Cover and let rise again until doubled in bulk. Brush top with beaten egg yolk and bake in oven at 425°F, mark 6, for 40 minutes, or until browned.

Baking Powder Brioche

½ *pound flour (sifted)*   *4 eggs*
½ *teaspoon salt*   *3 fluid ounces light ale*
2 ounces sugar   *6 ounces butter (softened)*
1 tablespoon baking powder

Have ready 24 well buttered brioche tins. Sift together flour, salt, sugar, and baking powder. Beat eggs until light and fluffy. Add flour mixture and light ale alternately to eggs, then beat in the butter. Cover and allow to stand in a cool place overnight* (not the refrigerator). Pre-heat oven to 375°F, mark 5, and bake for 15 minutes or until browned.

*The mixture may be baked after standing for 1 hour, but the longer it stands the better the flavour.

Yorkshire Parkin

1 pound plain flour   *2½ pounds treacle*
1 pound oatmeal (fine)   *2 eggs*
1 pound oatmeal (medium)   ½ *pint brown ale*
6 ounces lard   ½ *ounce ginger (ground)*
6 ounces butter   *2 teaspoons bicarbonate soda*

Rub the fat into the flour. Stir in the oatmeal and mix thoroughly. Warm treacle and stir into oatmeal mixture. Make a well in the centre; beat eggs; mix ginger, soda and beer together with eggs and drop into well. Stir until you have a well mixed very thick batter which will not run off the spoon. Pre-heat oven to 350°F, mark 4. Well grease 2 shallow baking tins and divide mixture between them, taking care to leave tins half-full. Bake parkins for ¾–1 hour.

Madeira Cake

13 ounces plain flour
10 ounces castor sugar
8 ounces butter
rind ½ lemon (grated)
5 eggs

1 teaspoon baking powder
8 fluid ounces old ale
slice candied citron peel
pinch salt

Heat the oven to 350°F, mark 4, and prepare an 8-inch diameter cake tin (*see* page 105). Cream butter, sugar and grated lemon rind in a bowl and beat until mixture is light. Add eggs with a tablespoon of flour one at a time. Sift remaining flour with baking powder and salt and stir into mixture with the beer. Turn into cake tin and cook in pre-heated oven for ½ hour. At the end of this time place citron on top to cook for a further 1 hour, reducing heat to 325°F, mark 3, after 30 minutes. To test if cake is done, lightly press the top with the fingertips. It should spring back if cooked.

Walnut and Cherry Cake

8 ounces self-raising flour
pinch salt
6 ounces butter
6 ounces castor sugar
3 eggs

4 ounces glacé cherries
  (halved)
2 ounces walnuts (chopped)
2 tablespoons old ale

Heat oven to 350°F, mark 4, and prepare cake tin (*see* page 105). Sift flour and salt together. Cream butter in a bowl with sugar. Beat eggs and whisk into the butter mixture. Mix 2 tablespoons of flour with the fruit and nuts. Fold flour into eggs and butter, a third at a time, adding fruit at the end. Mix with beer. Turn into cake tin and cook for 1 hour in pre-set oven. When cake is cooked a fine skewer inserted in it should come away clean.

Welsh Fruit Cake

1½ pounds plain flour	4 ounces sweet almonds
½ pound butter	(skinned and split)
1 pound castor sugar	½ nutmeg (grated)
¼ pound mixed peel	½ ounce yeast
½ pound currants	½ pint pale ale
½ pound raisins	juice ½ orange
½ pound sultanas	juice ½ lemon

Cream the yeast with the sugar and mix the flour in a bowl and when mixed rub in the fat before adding the sugar, fruit, nuts and fruit juice. Gradually mix in the pale ale taking care not to use it all if mixture looks like becoming too soft. Turn into a greased baking tin and bake in a moderate oven for 2½–3 hours.

Porter Plum Cake

½ pound butter or	¼ pound mixed dried peel
margarine	3 eggs
1 pound flour	½ teaspoon cinnamon
½ pound demarara sugar	½ teaspoon nutmeg (grated)
1 pound currants, raisins	½ pint sweet stout
or sultanas	1 teaspoon baking soda

Rub the fat, flour and sugar together in a bowl until well mixed. Add the fruit, dried peel, baking soda, cinnamon and nutmeg. Mix in the 3 eggs and gradually add the ½ pint of stout. If mixture looks like getting too wet do not use all the sweet stout. Pour into prepared cake tin (*see* page 105) and bake in a moderate oven, 325°F, mark 3, for 2½ hours.

Spiced Beer Cake

4 eggs
1 pound butter (or
  margarine)
½ pound dates (stoned and
  chopped)
1 pound sultanas or raisins
  (chopped)
2 pounds mixed nuts
  (chopped)
3 pounds plain flour
2½–3 pounds soft brown
  sugar
1 ounce salt

1 ounce baking powder
1 ounce bicarbonate soda
½ ounce allspice
  (powdered)
½ ounce ginger (powdered)
½ ounce cinnamon
  (powdered)
¼ ounce nutmeg or mace
  (powdered)
½ teaspoon cayenne pepper
¼ ounce cloves (powdered)
½ pint stout

Sift the flour, powders and spices in a large bowl and stir in the
fruit and nuts. Cream the fat, eggs and sugar in a separate bowl.
Mix all together using the beer to moisten but not drown the
mixture. Turn into a prepared cake tin (see page 105) and bake
in a moderate oven, 325°F, mark 3, for about 2½ hours.

Scots Gingerbread with Beer

8 ounces butter (or
  margarine)
4 ounces castor sugar
8 ounces black treacle
½ ounce ginger (ground)
½ teaspoon cloves (ground)
2 eggs
1 pound plain flour
4 ounces currants

4 ounces sultanas
1 teaspoon bicarbonate soda
3 ounces almonds (ground)
3 ounces candied peel
  (chopped)
½ ounce mixed spice
½ teaspoon cinnamon
  (ground)
8 fluid ounces strong ale

Cream the butter and sugar in a bowl. Slightly warm the treacle
and stir it in. Add the eggs and beat the mixture well. Sift the
flour with the spices and mix. Add fruit and nuts and bicarbonate
of soda. Add the beer gradually, taking care not to use all the

beer if the mixture looks like getting too wet. Put into a large prepared cake tin and bake in a moderate oven for 2 hours.

Highland Ginger Cake

½ pound butter (or margarine)	*1 pound flour*
¼ pound castor sugar	*½ ounce ground ginger*
½ pound black treacle	*½ ounce mixed spices*
2 eggs	*¼ pound mixed fruit*
¼ pint sweet stout	*3 ounces mixed peel*
	1 teaspoon baking soda

Cream the fat and sugar in a bowl. Add the treacle and eggs and gradually mix in the flour, ginger, spices, fruit and peel. Dissolve the baking soda in the beer and stir into the cake mixture, taking care not to let it become too soft. Turn into a well greased baking tin and bake for 2½ hours in a moderate oven at 325°F, mark 3.

Chocolate Layer Cake

3 ounces chocolate (unsweetened)	*¼ pound butter*
1½ cups plain flour	*¾ cup castor sugar*
pinch salt	*2 eggs*
6 fluid ounces brown ale	*2 egg whites*
1½ teaspoons baking powder	*4 ounces icing sugar*
pinch baking soda	*½ pound unsalted butter*

Well butter two 8-inch diameter sandwich tins and dust with flour. Heat oven to 350°F, mark 4. Cream the butter and sugar together and beat until fluffy. Melt the chocolate over hot water and leave to cool a little. Sift flour, salt, baking powder and baking soda together in a bowl. Add 1 egg to the butter mixture, beating well. Add second egg, beating again. Stir in ⅔ of the chocolate leaving enough to colour the butter cream. Add a little flour mixture, stirring in well and a little beer, continue adding beer and flour mixture in this way until all is used. Mix until smoothly blended. Turn into sandwich tins. Cook for about 25 minutes or until a

knitting needle inserted in the cakes comes out clean. Turn on to
a rack to cool. While cake rounds are cooling make the butter
cream. Whisk egg whites and icing sugar in a basin over hot
water until just stiff. Cream butter and add egg mixture to it, a
little at a time. Flavour with melted chocolate. Spread butter
cream on one round of layer cake and sandwich with second
round. Decorate top with butter cream rosettes or beer chocolate
icing (*see* below).

Chocolate Profiteroles

choux pastry with beer	*6 ounces bitter chocolate*
(see *éclairs—p. 116*)	$\frac{1}{2}$ *pint water*
$\frac{1}{2}$ *pint double cream*	*4 ounces granulated sugar*
(*whipped*)	

Prepare choux pastry in same quantity as for éclairs (*see* page
116). Pre-heat oven to 400°F, mark 6. Pipe pastry out in small
balls on to a dampened baking sheet and bake for 10 minutes
before turning oven up to 425°F, mark 7, for a further 15–20
minutes until crisp. Prick to release steam and leave to cool.
Whip cream and set aside. Meanwhile, make chocolate sauce.
Melt chocolate with water in a saucepan over a low heat. Add
sugar and when sugar is dissolved bring to the boil and simmer
uncovered for about 15 minutes until sauce is syrupy. Allow to
cool for a little. Make a slit in profiteroles and pipe in whipped
cream. Serve with chocolate sauce poured over.

Serves 4–6

Chocolate Icing

2 tablespoons butter	*2 cups castor sugar*
2 ounces chocolate	*2 tablespoons lager*
(*unsweetened*)	

Cream butter and sugar together. Melt chocolate and add to
mixture. Beat well. Stir in beer and continue to beat until smooth.
Delicious on plain sponge cakes or on chocolate layer cake (*see*
page 114).

Coffee Eclairs

2½ ounces plain flour
2½ fluid ounces light ale
2½ fluid ounces water
2 eggs
2 ounces butter

½ pint double cream
1–2 tablespoons coffee
  essence
¾ pound icing sugar

Pre-heat oven to 400°F, mark 6. First make the choux pastry. Put fat, beer and water in a large pan and bring to the boil. Remove pan from heat and when just off the boil pour in all the flour and stir vigorously. Allow mixture to cool for a few minutes before beating in eggs one at a time. (Mixture should remain firm and you may find that you do not need all of last egg if they are large eggs.) Beat pastry for a few minutes longer until it looks glossy. Pipe out in 4-inch lengths on to dampened baking sheets. Bake for 10 minutes in pre-heated oven then turn up to 425°F, mark 7, for a further 15 minutes. When éclairs are cooked they should be brown in colour—if too pale they will collapse. Prick sides to release steam and leave to cool. Whip cream and split éclairs ready to fill. Mix icing sugar with enough water to give the consistency of thick cream. Flavour with coffee essence. Fill éclairs with whipped cream. Warm icing, remove from heat and dip tops of éclairs into it. Leave to set before serving.

Makes éclairs for 4–6 people

Old English Biscuits

6 ounces flour
3 ounces butter
pinch salt
¼ teaspoon bicarbonate soda
¼ teaspoon vanilla essence

1 tablespoon old ale
1 egg (beaten)
2 ounces soft brown sugar
2 ounces castor sugar
¾ cup mincemeat

Sift flour, salt and soda together. Cream butter with sugar, beat till fluffy and add the egg. Sprinkle with a little of the flour then mix in the remaining flour. Moisten the mincemeat with the beer, taking care not to make it too wet. Add vanilla essence and stir into flour mixture. Grease a baking sheet and drop mixture in teaspoonfuls on to it a couple of inches apart. Pre-heat oven to 375°F, mark 5–6, bake for about 10 minutes.

Beer Fingers

2 ounces self-raising flour
2 ounces porridge oats
1 tablespoon brown sugar
1 teaspoon ginger (ground)

1 teaspoon cinnamon
¼ pint extra strong ale
pinch salt

Mix ingredients together thoroughly and make into a stiff paste with the ale. Pour mixture into a well-greased shallow baking tin and bake at 350°F, mark 4, for 20 minutes. When almost cool cut into fingers with a blunt buttered knife.

Lobster in Beer Sauce (*page 66*)

Possets, Punches and Other Beer Brews

FROM Piers Plowman and Chaucer, through Shakespeare and Johnson to the present age, poets and minstrels have sung the praises of beer and today we have inherited many superb beer-based drinks whose very names are fascinating: possets and punches, wassails and syllabubs; Het Pint or Figgy Sue, Tewah-diddle or Brown Betty.

Many of these drinks were drunk for medicinal purposes as well as pleasure. They undoubtedly did cure minor ailments such as colds and sore throats or backaches and headaches, even if they had little effect on the plague!

The following beer brews make superb party drinks and can be made in large quantities quite cheaply. But don't wait for a party occasion to try them. Nogs and toddies make lovely bed-time drinks, for instance, or, for a change, try a punch with your dinner.

Wassail

4 apples (small)
4 tablespoons brown sugar
2 cups light ale
$\frac{1}{4}$ teaspoon nutmeg (ground)
$\frac{1}{2}$ teaspoon cinnamon
  (ground)

$\frac{1}{4}$ teaspoon ginger (ground)
$\frac{1}{2}$ cup granulated sugar
$1\frac{1}{2}$ cups dry sherry

Ossi Bucchi (page 41)

Peel and slice apples. In a saucepan, heat the ale nutmeg, cinnamon, ginger, sugar and sherry. Stir until sugar is dissolved. Cook over low heat for 15 minutes, taking care not to let the mixture boil. Pour into a punch bowl and decorate with the apple rings.

Serves 6–8

Yard of Flannel

1 pint light ale
¼ cup sugar
4 tablespoons cognac

3 eggs (separated—
see p. 137)
½ teaspoon nutmeg (grated)

Combine sugar and cognac and stir until smooth. Beat the egg yolks until light in colour and beat the whites until stiff. Place the beer in a saucepan and heat until it barely begins to boil. Add the sugar mixture. Remove from heat. Add the beaten egg yolks and whites, and nutmeg and stir together. Pour into a large jug. Take another clean jug and pour mixture from one jug to another quickly but carefully, so as to induce the mixture to foam. The drink should be quite smooth.

Lamb's Wool

1 pint brown ale
1 cup apple sauce
¼ teaspoon ginger
(powdered)

¼ teaspoon vanilla extract
sugar to taste

Combine the ale and apple sauce in a saucepan and heat; remove from the heat just before boiling point. Add vanilla extract and ginger and stir well. Taste; for sweetening add a little sugar if necessary. Serve hot.

Serves 2

Bishop

2 pints light ale   *2 large oranges*
8 whole cloves   *1 tablespoon brown sugar*

Stick oranges with cloves. Bake in the oven at 250°F, mark 1, until very soft (about 25 minutes). Heat ale and sugar together in a saucepan. Cut each orange into 4 and remove seeds; add to the beer mixture. Remove from heat and let stand ½ hour. Heat again, but do not allow to boil. Serve hot with a piece of orange floating on top of each mug.

Serves 4–6

Figgy Sue

¼ pound dried figs   *1 tablespoon castor sugar*
1 pint water   *pinch ginger (ground)*
1 quart light ale

Wash figs and simmer in water in a saucepan until tender. Rub through a sieve. Heat the beer with the sugar and ginger and when nearly boiling add fig purée. Bring to the boil, stirring continuously and serve hot.

Serves 4

Mulled Ale

½ pint light ale   *¼ teaspoon grated nutmeg*
1 teaspoon honey

Place the honey in the bottom of a stone mug. Heat the ale or beer in a saucepan, without boiling. Pour over the honey and sprinkle with the nutmeg.

Danish Beer Toddy

¾ pint stout   *2 tablespoons brown sugar*
2 egg yolks

Heat the beer, but do not allow it to boil. Beat the egg yolks and sugar in a bowl. Gradually add the hot beer, stirring constantly. Return mixture to the saucepan and continue to stir. Re-heat, but do not allow to boil. If you like, sprinkle a little grated nutmeg on top of each serving.

Syllabub

2 cups brown ale   1½ quarts milk
2 cups cider   sugar to taste
½ cup seedless raisins
1½ teaspoons nutmeg or
    cinnamon (ground)

Pour boiling water over the raisins and let stand 30 minutes. Mix beer, cider, and milk together in a bowl. Leave to cool and beat with a rotary beater until foamy. Pour into a punchbowl. Drain the raisins and sprinkle over the mixture. Taste for sweetness the Syllabub and add a little sugar if necessary. Sprinkle with the cinnamon.

Serves 4–6

Beer Flip

2 pints strong ale   6 egg yolks
6 cubes sugar   2 tablespoons castor sugar
rind 1 lemon   ½ teaspoon nutmeg (grated)
½ teaspoon cinnamon

Rub the sugar cubes all round over the lemon rind until they turn yellow with zest and lemon rind goes 'bald'. Place all the ale, except for ½ pint, in a large saucepan with the sugar cubes and cinnamon. Bring to the boil slowly. Add remaining cold ale. Meanwhile beat egg yolks in a large jug with nutmeg and 2 tablespoons castor sugar and pour the hot ale on to the eggs, stirring all the time. Return mixture quickly to saucepan and back to jug a few times until a frothy head appears, when it is ready. Serve hot.

Serves 4–6

Beer Nog

1½ pints stout   ½ cup sugar
1 cup rum   4 eggs

Mix the rum, sugar and beer in a saucepan. Bring to the boil and
simmer 5 minutes. Remove from heat. Beat the eggs in a bowl
and gradually add the beer mixture, stirring steadily to prevent
curdling. Allow to chill in the refrigerator at least 2 hours. Before
serving, beat with a rotary beater.

Serves 2–3

Beer Punch

2 pints old ale   2 apples
4 cloves   ½ teaspoon nutmeg
½ teaspoon mixed spice   1 teaspoon sugar

Core and cut apples into slices but do not peel. Mix remaining
ingredients in a large saucepan. Add apples and heat through
slowly. Do not boil. Serve hot in tankards with apple slices on
top.

Raisin Punch

2 pints brown ale   rind 1 lemon
few coriander seeds   2 tablespoons brown sugar
  (crushed)   2 tablespoons raisins

Tie lemon rind and coriander seeds in a fine muslin bag. Pour
ale into a large saucepan and stir in sugar and raisins. Drop in
muslin bag and bring slowly to the boil. Simmer for about 10
minutes to infuse lemon rind and coriander flavourings. Remove
muslin bag and serve hot.

Serves 4

Spiced Beer

2 pints brown ale   3 cloves (whole)
¾ cup cognac   1¼ teaspoons ground cinnamon
2 eggs   ¼ teaspoon nutmeg
1 tablespoon sugar

Cool the beer and cognac and combine in a bowl with the sugar.
Beat the eggs well. Add with the cinnamon, cloves, and nutmeg
and mix together until well blended.

Serves 2–4

Ale Posset

4 eggs   3 whole cloves
4 tablespoons brown sugar   ¼ teaspoon ground
2 pints old ale   cinnamon

Heat the ale, sugar, cloves and cinnamon, taking care not to let
the mixture boil. Discard cloves. Beat the eggs in a bowl and
gradually add the ale mixture, stirring steadily. Return to the
heat and continue to stir. Beat with a rotary beater and serve hot
in mugs.

Serves 6–8

Christmas Eve Posset

2 pints brown ale   1 teaspoon cinnamon
4 cups milk   4 slices toast
4 tablespoons sugar

Heat sugar, milk and toast in a saucepan, taking care not to let
it boil. Stir the cinnamon and beer together in a punch bowl.
Discard toast and pour the hot milk over the ale. Stir. Serve hot
in mugs.

Serves 8

Spanish Posset

2 pints lager

2 slices toast

2 cups sherry

1 tablespoon brown sugar

1 tablespoon cinnamon

Butter the toast and sprinkle with sugar and cinnamon, pressing well in. Cut slices into quarters. Place toast, beer, and sherry in a saucepan and heat, taking care not to boil. Serve hot.

Serves 6–8

Russian Posset

1 cup light ale

1 teaspoon honey

Heat the beer and honey in a saucepan, but don't let it boil. Serve in glasses.

Tewahdiddle

½ pint light ale

2 teaspoons brandy

½ teaspoon brown sugar

1 slice lemon

¼ nutmeg (grated)

Stir the beer, brandy and sugar together until the sugar is dissolved. Pour into glass and add a slice of lemon. Grate the nutmeg over. Serve hot or cold.

Serves 1

Het Pint

2 quarts brown ale

2 eggs

1 egg yolk

1 nutmeg

sugar to taste

¼ pint whisky

Pour the ale into a large enamel saucepan. Add grated nutmeg. Bring to the boil and sweeten with sugar to taste. Beat the eggs with the egg yolk and slowly add the hot ale so as not to curdle. Stir in whisky. Return to saucepan and stir till nearly boiling, then pour it from a height into a tankard and continue to pour backwards and forwards from tankard to pan till it froths.

Serves 6

Ale Punch

2 quarts light ale   1 lemon
½ pint sherry   6 ice cubes
2 ounces castor sugar

Put the sugar in a punch bowl. Peel lemon rind as thinly as possible and add to sugar. Squeeze lemon juice and strain over sugar. Stand for ½ hour then remove lemon rind. Add ale, sherry and ice. Float lemon slices on top.

Serves 6

Brown Betty

2 pints light ale   3 cloves
1 cup cognac   ¼ cup brown sugar
¼ teaspoon cinnamon   2 cups water

Combine all the ingredients and mix well. Chill for 2 hours before serving.

Serves 6–8

Shandy Gaff

½ pint light ale (chilled)   ½ pint ginger beer (chilled)

Pour the beer and ginger ale simultaneously into a chilled glass.

Serves 1

Russian Beer

½ pint light ale   1 slice lemon
1 fluid ounce vodka

Combine the vodka and beer. Float slice of lemon on top.

Serves 1

Purl

½ pint old ale   dash bitters
1 fluid ounce gin

Heat the beer until it boils. Combine the gin and bitters in a mug
and pour the beer over it.

Serves 1

Dog's Nose

1½ fluid ounces gin   ½ pint lager (chilled)

Combine the gin and beer.

Serves 1

Brewer's Coffee

4 tablespoons coffee (fresh   whipped cream to serve
   ground)   sugar to taste
½ pint light ale

Place a tablespoon of coffee in each of 4 filters. Heat beer to
boiling point and pour into filters in place of water. Warm glasses
and place sugar to taste in the bottom. When coffee has dripped
through pour quickly into glass and serve with whipped cream
floating on top.

Serves 1

Miscellaneous Recipes

THE FOLLOWING are recipes which do not fit into any of the previous sections of the book, but which are both tasty and useful on many occasions.

Suffolk Sweet Cured Ham

ham as required
1 quart stout
1 quart vinegar
1 pound rock salt
1 pound granulated sugar
½ ounce saltpetre

1 pound kitchen salt
½ ounce peppercorns
½ ounce cloves
2 ounces hops
1 quart water

Boil hops in water for ½ hour. Strain and reserve liquid. Mix remaining ingredients, except ham, together in a large saucepan and bring to the boil. Add the hop water. Leave to cool. Place ham in a large shallow dish and pour mixture over. Baste daily, leaving to marinate for 3–6 weeks according to size of ham. Hang up to dry before storing.

Beer Cured Ham (1)

ham as required
½ pound kitchen salt
½ pound rock salt
2 ounces saltpetre
2 ounces juniper berries
  (crushed)

1 quart light ale
1 pound treacle
1 ounce black pepper
  (ground)
1 ounce allspice
  (powdered)

Mix all the ingredients together except the ham, and leave overnight to dissolve treacle. Stir and bring to the boil in a large
enamel saucepan. Place ham in a large stone crock and when
mixture has cooled pour over ham and rub well in. Cover and
leave to marinate for 4 weeks, basting each day. Hang in a cool
place to dry.

Beer Cured Ham (2)

ham as required	*¼ pound kitchen salt*
1 quart stout	*¼ pound demerara sugar*
¼ pound rock salt	*1 ounce saltpetre*

Hang ham for at least 3 days before curing. Mix remaining
ingredients together in a large enamel saucepan and bring to the
boil. Put ham in a large stone crock and pour hot mixture over.
Leave ham to marinate for 3 weeks, turning it a couple of times
a day.

Yorkshire Pudding

5 ounces plain flour	*pinch salt*
1 egg	*1 tablespoon beef suet*
¼ pint milk	*1 tablespoon dripping*
¼ pint light ale	

Mix beer and milk together. Mix flour and salt in a bowl and
make a well in the middle. Break egg into this and pour in half the
milk and beer. Stir carefully, drawing flour in gradually. Mix in
remaining beer, milk and suet and leave to stand for at least ½
hour before cooking. Heat dripping in a tin, tilting it to coat the
sides of the tin. Pre-heat oven 400°F, mark 7, and cook Yorkshire
pudding for 30–40 minutes on a high shelf.

Beer Puffs

1 cup light ale	*4 eggs*
1 cup self-raising flour	*½ teaspoon salt*
4 ounces butter	

Melt butter in a saucepan, add beer and bring to the boil. Mix in flour and salt and cook over low heat stirring continuously until mixture leaves sides of pan. Remove from heat and beat in eggs, one at a time. Have ready a baking sheet lined with buttered greaseproof paper and drop mixture on to this in teaspoonfuls, leaving enough space between each puff to allow for swelling. Bake in a pre-heated oven at 450°F, mark 7, for 10 minutes. Reduce heat to 350°F, mark 4, and cook for a further 10 minutes until brown. Allow to cool. Split and fill with cocktail filling of your choice, such as cheese mixture, liver paté, mushrooms in white sauce, etc.

Makes 36

Stuffed French Loaves

1 loaf French bread
½ pound cream cheese
¼ pint light ale
½ pound liver sausage
1 tablespoon English mustard (dry)

1 tablespoon onion (chopped)
1 tablespoon radishes (chopped)
1 tablespoon parsley (chopped)

Pre-heat oven to 350°F, mark 4. Cut bread lengthways into two pieces. Cut off ends and discard. Scoop out soft centre, crumble and lay aside. Mix cream cheese with beer, mustard and liver sausage. Stir in breadcrumbs and pack this mixture into bread halves. Press two halves together again firmly. Chill in refrigerator for about 4 hours and slice to serve.

Beer Scrambled Eggs

5 eggs
¼ pint milk
⅛ pint light ale

½ ounce butter
seasoning to taste
toast to serve

Break eggs into a bowl and beat until frothy. Add milk and beer and beat again. Melt butter in a saucepan and pour in egg mixture. Stir with a metal spoon over a high flame, continuously scraping mixture away from sides and bottom of pan until scrambled to the required consistency. Serve hot with toast and black pepper sprinkled over to taste.

Serves 2

Beer 'n Mustard Dip

¼ cup English mustard (dry)   1½ tablespoons vinegar
2 dessertspoons cornflour   1 dessertspoon castor sugar
½ pint light ale   1 teaspoon caraway seeds

Mix all the ingredients in a large saucepan and heat stirring continuously. Keep warm over a warming plate and serve with sausages to dip in.

Barbecue Sauce

½ pint brown ale   2 teaspoons sugar
½ pint chilli sauce   2 tablespoons Worcestershire
1 medium onion (grated)   sauce
2 tablespoons vinegar   2 teaspoons chilli powder

Combine all ingredients in a saucepan, bring to boil and cook 3 minutes. Delicious as basting sauce for spare ribs, chicken, Frankfurters, etc.

Chinese Barbecue Sauce

¾ pint stout   4 drops Tabasco sauce
½ teaspoon salt   2 tablespoons sugar
1 tablespoon mustard   4 tablespoons orange
1 teaspoon ginger (ground)   marmalade
3 tablespoons soy sauce   2 cloves garlic (minced)

Combine all the ingredients in a bowl. Use as marinade for spare ribs of pork, lamb chops, chicken or ham before barbecuing or grilling the meat.

Cheese Sauce

7 ounces Cheddar cheese
 (grated)
1 tablespoon butter
¼ pint light ale
1 teaspoon Worcestershire
 sauce

½ teaspoon salt
½ teaspoon mustard
dash cayenne pepper

Combine cheese and butter in top of a double boiler and place over hot water until cheese begins to melt. Gradually add light ale, stirring until smooth. Stir in remaining ingredients. Use with asparagus, broccoli, hard-boiled eggs, etc.

Mushroom Sauce (1)

4 tablespoons butter
1 onion (minced)
½ pound mushrooms
 (peeled and sliced)

¾ teaspoon salt
2 tablespoons flour
¾ pint sweet stout

Sauté the onion and mushrooms in the butter for 10 minutes. Sprinkle with salt and flour, gradually adding the stout and stirring constantly to boiling. Then cook 5 minutes more over low heat. Serve with steak or chops.

Mushroom Sauce (2)

3 tablespoons butter
1 large onion (minced)
½ pound mushrooms
 (peeled and sliced)

2 tablespoons flour
½ teaspoon salt
dash cayenne pepper
¾ pint sweet stout

Sauté the onions lightly in melted butter, add mushrooms and cook for another 3 minutes. Sprinkle in flour, salt and pepper, then gradually stir in the stout. Cook over low heat for 10 minutes, stirring frequently. Particularly suitable for steak and hamburgers.

Sweet Orange Sauce

¼ *pint light ale*   ¼ *pound brown sugar*
¼ *pint orange juice*   2 *tablespoons butter*
1 *tablespoon orange rind*
  (grated)

Combine all ingredients in a saucepan and cook, stirring occasionally, until syrupy. Serve on plain cakes, pancakes, ice-cream, etc.

Beer Hard Sauce

¼ *pound unsalted butter*   3 *tablespoons lager*
2 *ounces sugar*

Cream together the butter and sugar and blend in the beer. Chill. Serve with apple or other fruit pie, or plum pudding.

New England Pilgrims' Syrup

½ *pint brown ale*   ½ *pound brown sugar*

Mix beer and sugar and cook over low heat for 15 minutes, until syrupy. Serve hot or cold with pancakes, waffles, etc.

Fritter Batter

4 *ounces flour (sifted)*   ½ *pint lager*
½ *teaspoon salt*   2 *tablespoons butter (melted)*
2 *eggs (separated—see*
  p. 137)

Sift flour and salt into bowl. Beat egg yolks and stir in beer. Add to the flour, stirring only until blended, then add butter and allow to stand for 1 hour. Beat egg whites until stiff but not dry and fold into yolk mixture. Use for seafood, chicken or vegetables.

Yeast Fritter Batter

$\frac{1}{2}$ pint lager
1 teaspoon yeast powder
2 ounces lukewarm water
$\frac{1}{4}$ pound flour

pinch salt
1 tablespoon salad oil
1 egg white (stiffly beaten)

Heat beer slightly. Soften yeast in water. Combine flour and salt in a bowl; make well on centre and drop yeast into it. Work in flour and gradually add beer and oil. Beat for 2 minutes. The batter should have the consistency of thick cream; if not add a little water. Cover and set aside for 45 minutes. Just before using fold in egg white. Use for vegetables, meat or fish. For sweet batter add $1\frac{1}{2}$ teaspoons sugar. Dip selected food into batter and deep fry in hot oil or fat until browned.

Cocktail Frankfurters

2 pounds cocktail
  Frankfurters
1 14-ounce bottle tomato
  ketchup

$\frac{1}{2}$ pint light ale
dash Worcestershire sauce
3 tablespoons butter

Mix all the ingredients in a small saucepan, apart from the Frankfurters. Simmer gently for 1 hour. Add Frankfurters and heat through. Serve in a chafing dish, kept hot, for a delicious party dish.

Serves 12

Basic Hints

ALMONDS—skinning and shredding

To skin almonds easily pour boiling water over them and leave to cool. The skins can then be pressed off with the fingers. To shred them: first skin, then split in two and cut lengthways into fine pieces.

BREADCRUMBS

White crumbs: Cut the crust off a stale white loaf and reserve. Break bread up into crumbs by working through a sieve or electric blender. Spread on a sheet of paper and leave to dry for at least 2 days in a warm place, such as an oven warming drawer, before using or storing in a jam jar.

Browned crumbs: bake the bread crust in a low oven until golden and then crush finely before using or storing.

CHICKEN—trussing

The simplest and quickest way to truss a chicken is to put a skewer through the bird below the thigh bone, turn it on to its breast and catch in the wing pinions with string. Pass the string under the ends of the skewer and cross wing pinions over its back. Turn bird over again and bring string up to secure drumsticks, tying ends round the 'parson's nose'.

EGGS—separating

Crack the egg shell carefully and holding the egg with both hands over a bowl open the split just enough to allow the white to drip through. Rotate the egg carefully to allow white from all sides to escape into the bowl without breaking the yolk.

OMELET

3 eggs	*salt and pepper*
½ ounce butter	

Beat eggs lightly with salt and pepper to taste. Heat omelet pan and melt butter, making sure that the whole of the sides and base of the pan are covered with melted butter. Put egg mixture in pan and allow to cook slowly, stirring until eggs begin to set. When cooked, fold over and slide on to hot plate. If cooking a number of omelets, keep in pan in warm oven between cookings.

PASTRY—shortcrust

8 ounces plain flour	*pinch salt*
4 ounces butter	*3–4 tablespoons cold water*
2 ounces lard	

Sift flour and salt into a mixing bowl and cut butter and lard into flour. Rub in with fingers until mixture looks like fine breadcrumbs. Make a well in the centre and add 3 tablespoons water. Mix in with a knife to a firm dough, adding remaining water if necessary. Turn on to a floured board and knead lightly. Chill before using.

PASTRY—suet crust

8 ounces self-raising flour	*pinch salt*
6 ounces suet (shredded)	*cold water to mix*

Sift flour and salt in a bowl and stir in suet. Mix to a firm dough with about 4 fluid ounces of cold water. Knead lightly and roll out to a circle about 1 inch thick for steak and kidney pudding, etc.

STOCK

Use 3 pounds of beef, chicken or veal bones or a mixture of all three, depending on type required. Dry fry for 15–20 minutes then add peeled and diced vegetables to pan (eg 2 onions, 2 carrots, stick of celery). When bones and vegetables are just coloured add a few peppercorns, bouquet garni, seasoning and 3–4 quarts water. Bring to the boil slowly, simmering from time to time, then cover pan and simmer for 4–5 hours when stock should be well reduced. Strain off. Bones can be used again to make a second weaker stock.

Glossary of Cookery Terms

Bain-marie, au To cook just below boiling point in pot etc standing in a pan of simmering water, in oven or on top of stove.

Bake-blind To pre-cook a pastry case before filling with fruit, etc. This is done by lining the pastry case with greaseproof paper and filling with rice or beans to keep its shape before baking in the usual way.

Blanch To remove very strong taste from vegetables, fruit rind, etc., by placing in cold water, bringing to the boil and draining.

Bouquet garni Mixed herbs (traditionally thyme, parsley and bay leaf) tied in a bunch.

Butter, clarified Butter which has been heated and the milk solids skimmed from it and discarded.

Butter, kneaded Butter and flour kneaded together to a paste. Use twice as much butter as flour.

Croûtes Rounds of fried or toasted bread.

Croûtons Diced croûtes.

Flour, seasoned Flour to which salt and pepper have been added.

Larding strips Strips of bacon fat cut about $1\frac{1}{2}$ inches long and $\frac{1}{4}$ inch thick. They are sewn into very lean meat to give extra fat.

Liaison Thickening/binding mixture for soups, gravies, sauces, etc. (e.g. egg yolks, cream, roux, kneaded butter).

Luting paste A paste of flour and water used to seal the lid of a terrine to prevent steam escaping when paté is being cooked.

Marinate To soak raw meat or fish in a given mixture of spiced liquid/beer/wine/herbs, etc., for hours or days before cooking.

Reduce To boil down gravy or sauce to concentrate flavour and thicken the consistency.

Roux A butter and flour liaison used in the proportions given in the individual recipe.

Sauté To brown food in butter, or oil and butter.

Seasoning Salt and pepper.

Index

ALE:
  'bid', ix
  'bride', ix
  'clerk', ix
  'give', ix
  Mild or Brown, viii
  Mulled, 121
  Old, viii
  Pale, viii
  'Whitsun', ix
Apple Dragons, 99
Asparagus Parmesan, 71
Avocados Roquefort, 9

BACON, SWEET BOILED, 35–6
Banana Welsh Rarebit, 84
Bass, Boiled in Beer, 64
Batter:
  Fritter, 134
  Yeast Fritter, 135
Beans, Beer and Treacle, 75–6
Beef:
  Marinated in Beer, 21
  Pot Roast of, 25
  Stewed in Beer, 20–1
Beef Sausage, Alsace, 30
Beer:
  Burgers, 27–8
  Fingers, 117
  Flip, 122
  Nog, 123
  Puffs, 130–1
  Russian, 126
  Spiced, 124
Biftek à la Bière, 23–4

Biscuits, Old English, 116–17
Bishop, 121
Bortsch, Beer, 4–5
Bread:
  Beer, 106–7
  Date-nut, 108–9
  Sour Rye, 108
  Swedish Limpa, 107–8
Brioche:
  Baking Powder, 110
  Cheese, 109–10
Brown Betty, 126
Brussels Sprouts in Beer, 72
Buckinghamshire Florentine, viii, 98

CABBAGE, BRAISED AMSTERDAM, 71
Cake:
  Chocolate Layer, 114–15
  Highland Ginger, 114
  Madeira, 111
  Porter Plum, 112
  Spiced Beer, 113
  Walnut and Cherry, 111
  Welsh Fruit, 112
Carbonnade, 18–19
Carbonnades des Flamandes, vii, 17
Carp:
  Braised, in Beer, 63
  Spiced, in Beer, 63
  with Gingerbread, 64
Carrots in Beer, 72
Casserole:
  Beef and Mustard, 19–20

142   INDEX

Casserole—*cont.*
  Chilli, 23
  Farmhouse, 20
  Gammon, 36
  Lamb, 38
  Pork, 32
Cassoulet, 75
Cauliflower au Gratin, 74
Cheese:
  and Bacon Creams, 90
  Camembert, Home-made, 86
  Chive and Parsley, 86
  Cones, 92–3
  Dips, 88, 89
  Gloucester, in Ale, 86
  Gouda Puffs, 92
  Pancakes, 93
  Potted, 87
Cheese Balls, Danish, 91–2
Cheesecake, with Beer, 103
Cheese Muff, 84
Cheese Spread, Australian, 88
Chicken:
  and Beer Pilaf, 44
  Flemish Style, 43
  Fried, Kent, 45
  Mexican, with Rice, 43–4
  Roast, Italian, 45–6
  Sauté Marengo, 46
  Spring, Stew, 44–5
Chicory Mornay, 11–12
Chocolate Icing, 115
Christmas Pudding:
  Rich, 96
  Spicy, 97
Cod Fries, 61–2
Coffee, Brewer's, 127
Coleslaw, German, 77
Courgettes in Beer, 74
Crême Bonbel, 87–8
Croque, Beer and Bacon, 91

Date delight, 98
Dog's Nose, 127
Dressing:
  Beer (for Potato Salad), 80
  Coleslaw, 79

Lager, 79–80
Duck:
  Casserole with Rice, 46–7
  Ragout of, 47
Duckling, Salmis of, 47–8

Eclairs, coffee, 116
Eels, in Beer, 62
Eggs:
  Baked, in Beer, 14
  Poached, with Beer Sauce, 12–13
  Scrambled, Beer, 131–2
English Monkey, 84

Figgy sue, 121
Fish:
  Beer Batter for, 61
  Beer Sauce for, 54
Flan, Vanilla Cream, 100
Flapjacks, 102
Fondue, Beer, 85
Frankfurters:
  and Sauerkraut, 30
  Cocktail, 135
  in Beer Sauce, 29, 30
Fritters:
  Beer and Banana, 102–3
  Peach, 102
  Potato, 70
Fruits de Mer à la Bière, 66

Gammon casserole, 36
Gingerbread, Scots, with Beer, 113–14
Gouda Cheese Puffs, 92
Goulash with Beer, 27

Halibut in lager, 58
Ham:
  Baked, with Pineapple, 35
  Beer Cured, 129, 130
  Suffolk Sweet Cured, 129
  Sweet Boiled, 34, 35
Hare, Jugged, 51–2
Herrings:
  Baked, 60
  Soused, 60

Het Pint, 125
Hush Puppies, 109

KASE, BIER, 87

LAGER, viii
Lamb:
   Braised, with Stout, 37
   Casserole, 38
   Curried, 37–8
   Kebabs, 38
   Roast Leg of, 37
Lamb's Wool, 120
Lancashire Rarebit, 83
Liaison (thickening), 139
Liver, with Beer, 42
Loaf, Savoury Meat, 28
Loaves, Stuffed French, 131
Lobster in Beer Sauce, 66

MAIDEN'S PROVING, 57–8
Meatballs, with Beer, 28–9
Meat Loaf, Savoury, 28
Melon:
   Cocktail, 9
   in Beer, 8–9
Mexican Rarebit, 81–2
Mustard Rarebit, 83

OMELET, BEER, 13
Onions, Beer-batter, 70
Orange Sauce, 48
Ox Tail, Stewed, 42–3

PANCAKES:
   Danish, 100
   French, 101
   Viennese, 100–1
Parkin, Yorkshire, 110
Partridge Casserole, 48–9
Peach and Pear Salad, 99
Peach Trifle, 99
Peppers, Stuffed, 73–4
Pheasant, Stuffed, 49–50
Piperade, with Beer, 1, 9–10
Plaice, Beer Baked, 57
Pork:
   Braised, in Beer, 31

Casserole, 32
Chops, in Ale, 33–4
Chops, with Sauerkraut, 32
Fillets, in Brown Ale, 32–3
Roast, in Beer and Herbs, 33
Possett:
   Ale, 124
   Christmas Eve, 124
   Russian, 126
   Spanish, 125
Pot Roast, Brewer's, 22
Potatoes, Beer, 71
Prawns:
   in Beer, 65
   Stuffed, 65
Profiteroles, Chocolate, 115
Punch:
   Ale, 126
   Beer, 123
   Raisin, 123
Purl, 127

QUICHE, BEER, 1
Quiche Lorraine à la Bière, 12

RAISIN PUDDING, 97
Rarebit:
   Banana Welsh, 84
   Lancashire, 83
   Mexican, 81–2
   Mustard, 83
   Shrimp, 82
   Welsh, vii, 81
   Worcester, 82
Ratatouille, Beer, 76
Ribs, New World, 29

SALAD:
   Celery, Olive and Raisin, 78
   French Bean, 78
   Mushroom, in Beer, 79
   Potato, with Beer Dressing, 77
   Susannah, 76
Sallé, 90
Salmon, Braised, 54–5
Sauce:
   Barbecue, 132

Sauce—*cont.*
  Beer, Hard, 134
  Cheese, 133
  Chinese Barbecue, 132
  Mushroom, 133
  Sweet Orange, 134
Sausage Casserole, Beer and, 31
Scallops, Hungarian, 67
Seafood:
  Mixed, with Rice, 67
  Salad, 68
Shandygaff, 126
Shrimp Rarebit, 82
Shrimps:
  Hors d'Oeuvres, Hot, 14
  in Beer, 65
Skate au Gratin, 59
Sole:
  Baked, Fillet of, 55–6
  Casserole of, 56–7
  Dover, au Gratin, 55
  in Ginger Sauce, 56
Soup:
  Beer au Fromage, 6–7
  Beer, with Milk, 7
  Beer, with Prawn, 6
  Breakfast Beer, 4
  French Beer, 5–6
  German Cold Ale, 8
  Iced Cucumber, 8
  Lentil, with Beer, 3
  Norwegian Cold Ale, 7
  Scots Pheasant, 5
  Spring, 3
  Vegetable Beer, 2
Spare Ribs, Barbecued in Beer, 11
Steak:
  Chasseur, Stewed, 19
  in Ale, 24–5
  Rump, Charlie's, 23
  Rump, German, with Beer, 24
  Stewed, and Mushrooms, 25–6
Steak and Kidney Pie, 26–7

Steak and Kidney Pudding, 22
Stout, viii
Sweet Potato:
  Candied, 73
  Hawaiian, 73
  Soufflé, 72
Syllabub, 122
Syrup, New England Pilgrims', 134

TERRINE:
  Beer, 10–11
  Rabbit, 10
Tewahdiddle, 125
Toast, French Beer, 91
Toddy, Danish Beer, 121–2
Tomatoes, Party Beer, 78–9
Tripe in Ale, 42
Trout:
  Fillets of, in Beer, 59
  in Beer, 59

VEAL:
  Breast of, in Beer, 39
  Chops Sauté à la Bière, 41
  Escalopes de Veau à la Bière, 40
  Ossi Bucchi, 41
  Roast Loin of, 40–1
  Stuffed Shoulder of, 39
Vegetables, Beer Batter for, 69
Venison:
  Chasseur, 51
  Marinated, 50
Vol-au-Vents, Shrimp, 15

WAFFLES, BEER, 101
Wassail, 119–20
Welsh Rarebit, vii, 81
Whiting, Dijonnaise, 54
Worcester Rarebit, 82

YARD OF FLANNEL, 120
Yorkshire Pudding, 130